# How to Read Blueprints

Self instruction in the Language of Blueprints, Alphabet of the Lines, what is meant by Working and Assembly Drawings and how the two are used in a machine shop

By W. CLYDE LAMMEY

Copyright 1942
POPULAR MECHANICS COMPANY
CHICAGO

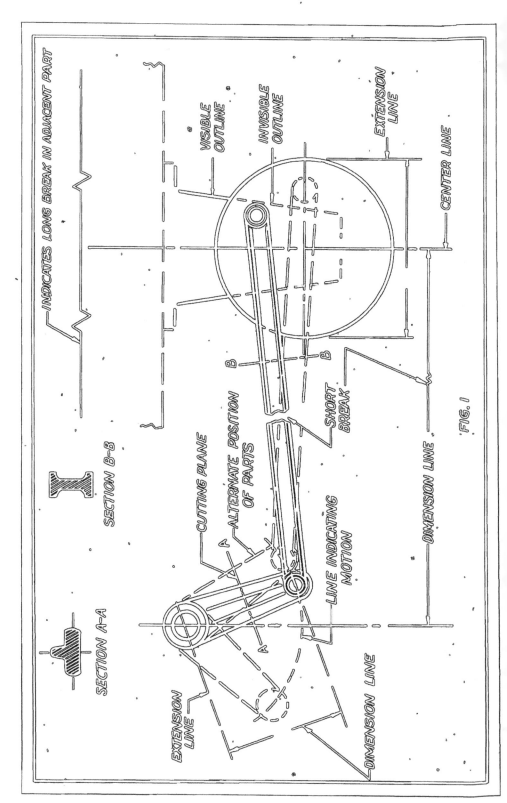

INDICATES LONG BREAK IN ADJACENT PART

VISIBLE OUTLINE

INVISIBLE OUTLINE

EXTENSION LINE

CENTER LINE

SECTION B-B

SECTION A-A

CUTTING PLANE

ALTERNATE POSITION OF PARTS

SHORT BREAK

LINE INDICATING MOTION

DIMENSION LINE

EXTENSION LINE

DIMENSION LINE

FIG. 1

# How to Read Blueprints

READING a blueprint is much like reading shorthand. You must understand the separate meanings of signs, symbols, and lines. The particular sign, the type of symbol and the weights and types of lines used on the blueprint—all these tell a story to the machinist, just as does a music score to the musician, or a weather chart to the airman. In reading a blueprint the machinist usually notes first the location and directions of the heavy lines which show the visible outline of the object, then the dotted lines which indicate the location of parts which are invisible in the assembly. Certain full lines in parallel, dotted lines, dot-dash lines or combinations of these tell him what kind of material is to be used and where it is to be located. Other lines will give the over-all dimensions, and, where necessary, the limit dimensions, and a note on the blueprint will indicate the scale reductions to which the object is drawn. If there is a repetition of parts and dimensions, the print will state how many duplicates in parts, what dimensions are duplicates, and will completely detail only one unit or its separate parts. If the object is irregular in shape the blueprint sometimes includes a perspective view to define the project more clearly in its several dimensions. Generally, projected front, side, and top or bottom views are used and sometimes these are subdivided and projected separately to make more clear to the machinist just what is to be done. Often prints detailing objects of complicated assembly will include a "bill of material" along with projected views, the parts of which are keyed with numbers or letters registering or corresponding with those on the material list so that the amount, size, and kind of materials used in the various parts can be more readily identified and calculated.

Looking at Fig. 1 and then at Fig. 2, the "alphabet" of lines, you will see how the draftsman puts these general rules into practice. Fig. 1 represents no particular

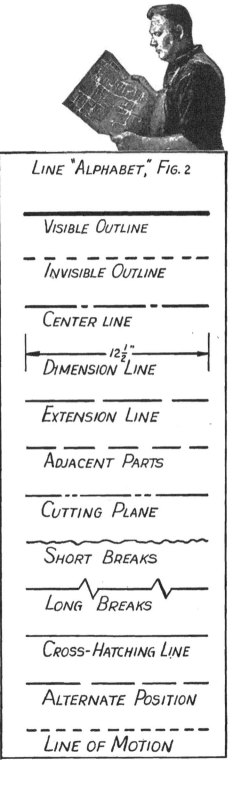

LINE "ALPHABET," FIG. 2

VISIBLE OUTLINE

INVISIBLE OUTLINE

CENTER LINE

$12\frac{1}{2}''$
DIMENSION LINE

EXTENSION LINE

ADJACENT PARTS

CUTTING PLANE

SHORT BREAKS

LONG BREAKS

CROSS-HATCHING LINE

ALTERNATE POSITION

LINE OF MOTION

mechanical device, nor are any of the parts dimensioned, but you will see at once how the visual representations of lines are carried out. Connecting it up with the line alphabet, Fig. 2, notice first how the visible outline, Fig. 1, is made to stand out by use of heavy lines. These lines have been purposely slightly exaggerated for the sake of emphasis. And note too, that the drawing, Fig. 1, makes use of all the lines shown in Fig. 2. Extension lines from the outline of parts terminate the dimension lines, long dash lines show the alternate position of moveable parts, lines consisting of alternating long and short dashes locate the centers, another consisting of a long dash and two short ones locates the cutting planes, while a line of short dashes indicates the line of motion. A wavy line shows the position of short breaks in parts of the mechanism, while a straight line broken at more or less regular intervals into a zigzagged section shows the location of long breaks. The draftsman uses the latter two lines to indicate that a section of the mechanism or part has been "broken away" for convenience in making the drawing or that in general, it is not essential that it be fully shown. Thus the short break in the connecting rod in Fig. 1, simply means that the rod is not shown in its full length, while the long break would indicate that the full outline of the base or overhead support to which the mechanism is to be attached is not important or that it is too large to be conveniently shown in connection with the mechanism itself. Cutting-plane lines such as A-A and B-B, Fig. 1, are used by the draftsman to indicate that figuratively the part has been cut in two at the point where the line crosses it and that elsewhere on the print you will find an end or sectional view as is the case in Fig. 1, sectional views A-A and B-B. These show the contours or outlines of the parts viewed endwise. One thing to keep in mind in connection with breaks in dimensioned parts: The dimension given always indicates the full length. Sometimes when the nature of the drawing makes it necessary or where the indication of the break is more or less obscure, the draftsman may, for the sake of emphasis, indicate the break in the dimension line also, as in Fig. 1 Otherwise, indicating a break in the dimension line generally is considered unnecessary.

Another point that comes up here in connection with the detailing of the imaginary mechanism in Fig. 1, is that wha appear to be discrepancies in the relatic of the outline to the dotted lines indicatir alternate positions are generally ignore in making the mechanical drawing. Fo example, were the drawing made in i true proportion and if the relation of th parts in alternate positions were trul shown, then obviously you would see th dotted or dash lines indicating the alter nate positions in a slightly different posi tion on the print.

To visualize what is meant by this, thin of the connecting rod, Fig 1, as being twic as long as it is actually shown on the draw ing. Of course, the dotted lines indicatin its alternate position would not be in th location you see them.

The point here is that the blueprint i first and fundamentally a means of showi ing the required number of parts of a uni or machine in just sufficient detail to en able the draftsman to dimension it full; that is, give its size by means of dimen sioned drawings. That's really one simp' definition of what machinists and engineer call a "working" drawing, which term means simply that the machinist can wor directly from the drawing and build th object, unit, or machine without any infor mation other than that given on the prin or set of prints, as the case may be.

It should be kept in mind that the abov applies to only the one type of blueprin namely one showing what is referred t as a working drawing.

Hence, to sum up this phase of the dis cussion, certain details are treated a merely supplementary by the draftsma They are needed only to clarify the "pic ture," to aid one's eye and mind in visual izing, where this is at all necessary, wha the object actually looks like and for wha purpose it is intended.

To illustrate, go back again to Fig. 1. A a glance one learns that this could repre sent an overhead-mounted mechanism de signed for the purpose of changing a rotar motion to an oscillating or rocking motio by means of a pitman and pitman whee the latter mounted on a shaft which turr in hangers attached to the ceiling or a overhead beam or some other similar sup port, as indicated by the long break.

We know that the pitman is longer than it is.shown because of the short break. We know, too, that the sectional size of both the pitman and the crank arm is of no critical dimensional importance because only one sectional view of each is shown, sections A-A and B-B.

These are a few of the interpretations one accustomed to reading blueprints would get from the details in Fig. 1. However, bear in mind that this is not a blueprint of either the working, assembly, or location type. It is merely an imaginary, explanatory drawing showing common line usage. And there are variations from the general usage, as many manufacturers find it necessary, for special reasons, to adapt standard usage to their own particular needs. However, more and more effort is being directed to standardizing practice insofar as is possible.

One more point in connection with Fig. 1 has to do with the position of the eye in relation to the drawing. Primarily, the common mechanical drawings are simply the so-called "flat" views, that is, only that portion of the object lying in the same plane as the paper on which it is drawn, is shown. To put it another way, you actually see the object in only one of its several dimensions. In this way the mechanical drawing made of any part differs from the perspective drawing of the same part, for in the perspective view a solid object or surface is conceived of and represented as not lying in that surface or plane, but is delineated by means of a drawing in several planes, the procedure calculated to represent the object as it would appear to the eye when the object is placed at a given point, generally taken to be slightly below eye level for purposes of convenience.

However, the definition for the flat view is not literally true as you will see from another examination of Fig. 1. Obviously, the pitman disk or wheel and the shaft hanger which supports it and the shaft, do not lie in the same plane, that is, on the surface of the paper, although they are so represented. How do we know? Because of the lines, the symbolic meaning of which is the "language" of the blueprint.

Here the draftsman, for purposes of clarity, has labelled the lines. Ordinarily, of course, he does not do so on the orthodox blueprint. But here the solid line indicates the visible outline and the dash line the invisible outline. Note here the variation in the length of the dashes, of the various broken lines in Figs. 1 and 2. Even the variations have meaning. And from this we know that the portion of the hanger outlined by dash lines is invisible, that is, it is behind the pitman wheel and therefore a portion of it is obscured from view.

Here again is an example of the importance of study of the line alphabet. On the drawing, remember, the draftsman does not label these lines as you see them in Fig. 1. He depends on the blueprint reader to know the meaning of all the lines, symbols and terms he uses. For example, in Fig. 1, he proceeds on the assumption that your knowledge of the meaning or significance of lines will tell you that a portion of the shaft hanger is invisible from your viewpoint or "eye point," but he also depends on you to notice that the long-dash lines indicate a second or alternate position of the pitman, rod, and crank-arm assembly, and do not indicate that these parts are invisible to you. The lines tell the story.

And still it should be remembered that these parts, in flat views, are nearly always represented as lying in the same plane as the paper on which they are drawn. If they were not, then in Fig. 1, even from the same "eye-point," you would see a portion of the left-hand edge of both the pitman wheel and the hanger; you also would see another dimension of the crank arm and a slightly more relieved view of the pitman rod. All of which would convey to you more graphically the inference that these parts are solids, that is, they have not only length and width, but depth as well.

However, there are still exceptions. Sometimes where the purpose of clarity and simplicity will be served without sacrificing accuracy of interpretation, the draftsman shades such parts as the pitman, pitman wheel and crank arm to give the relief and depth of a solid.

When the necessity for more than one dimensioned view is apparent the draftsman usually follows the common practice of projecting the part, or parts, or the whole into three views, a side, top, and end view. These are generally dimensioned separately. Sometimes only two views are necessary to dimension the part fully. The method is frequently referred to as "third-

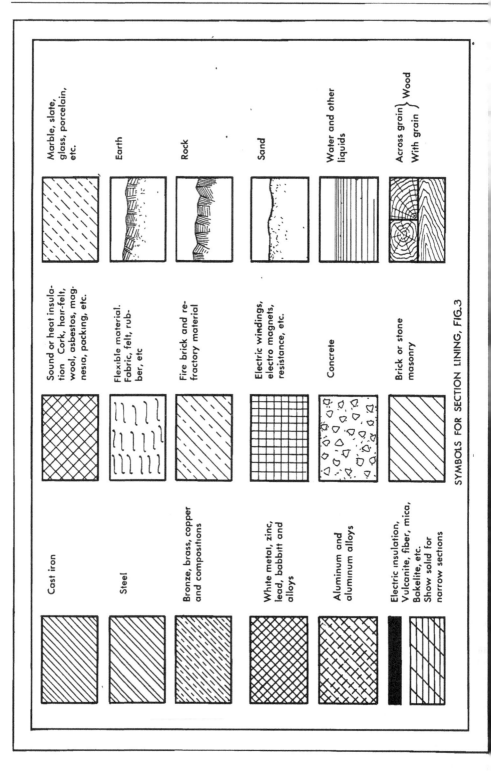

SYMBOLS FOR SECTION LINING, FIG.3

angle" projection. And there can be many variations in the location of the views as necessity and clarity require. Farther on this will be discussed more fully. Now to sum up, in mechanical drawings presenting dimensioned parts in flat views it is generally assumed that the object is viewed as it would appear when seen from above or from the side, in other words, you are looking down on the paper from a point centrally and directly above it. And in this position you actually see only two dimensions, length and width. When the part has been projected you see length, width and depth, but on separate drawings presenting different surfaces of the same object. To avoid confusion it is essential for both tyro and student to get this clearly in mind.

## Shop Terms:

It's worth one's time to devote a considerable study to the simple "dictionary" of shop terms included herewith. Only the most general terms are given and it sometimes happens that certain of these are given somewhat different meanings in shops doing work of a more or less specialized nature. Often you will find terms on blueprints, less the definitions, and it is up to you to quickly and accurately read their meaning. Now the important thing in these definitions is not just learning the words so that you could repeat the definition at once on seeing any given term. The blueprint reader and the machinist must know what is meant and what processes and tools must be used to accomplish the requirements of the specification.

As a random example, the blueprint specifies that certain holes drilled in a machine casting or other irregular-shaped part be "spot-faced" to seat the head of a given size capscrew. The machinist knows at once that the object of spot-facing the holes is to provide a true, flat surface for the machined head of the capscrew so that it may be drawn tight without developing a condition of strain which might break the head of the screw or warp or twist the machine part out of true during assembly. The definition mentions only a circular spot and although this is generally the case, it sometimes happens that the shape of the work makes it necessary to mill a flat surface on a rounded portion of the casting or

other part. In this case the "spot" is not truly circular but may be roughly semi-circular or triangular in shape. However, inasmuch as the work is generally done with an end milling cutter for the purpose of providing a flat surface for seating the head of a capscrew or bolt head it comes under the definition of spot-facing. As you will see, some of the terms are simply generally accepted names for machine parts; others describe and define common machine and hand-tool operations.

## Symbolic Section Linings:

When it is necessary to call special attention to, or to more clearly identify certain sectional parts which are made of different materials, and when these must be shown either in partial assembly or adjacent to one another on the drawing, the draftsman identifies the various materials by means of symbolic section lining or cross-hatching which consists generally of fine lines drawn in various patterns to represent different materials, as you see in Fig. 3.

Here the standards set up for drafting-room practice allow the draftsman considerable latitude as you see that one line pattern often can refer to several materials of a similar classification. And also, if he is distinguishing between various materials shown in separate views on the drawing the draftsman may, if he prefers, make the section lining simply by drawing equally spaced full lines in one direction. And in this case an opening is left in the section lining in which is placed a reference letter or number refering to a bill of materials. Or he may letter the name of the material in the opening provided. And often, when showing sectional views of parts of various materials adjacent to one another or in customary assembly views, it is desirable to use the symbolic section lining and include a reference letter which indicates the exact material to be used, or a reference to heat treatment or some other special information of importance. This will usually be given in a material list or will be specified on the print as a separate note. Aside from indicating materials alone, section-lining symbols have another value, although this is subsequent to the primary purpose. They have what

(Continued to page 11)

# A 'Dictionary'

**Anneal:** To soften metal by heating it to a critical temperature and allowing it to cool very slowly.

**Bore:** To enlarge a hole with a boring tool in a lathe or boring mill.

**Boss:** An integral part projecting from a casting or forging.

**Braze:** To join parts by use of hard solders.

**Broach:** To finish the inside of a hole, generally to a shape other than round. A tool used for this purpose.

**Buff:** To polish with a cloth wheel loaded with fine abrasive or polishing rouge.

**Burnish:** To polish with a rolling or sliding tool which is kept under pressure.

**Bushing:** A bearing sleeve or liner which is removable.

**Carburize:** To prepare a low carbon steel for heat treating by packing with carbonized material and heating to approximately 2,000 degrees for several hours, then cooling slowly.

**Case Harden:** To harden the surface of carburized steel by heating it to a critical temperature and then quenching it in an oil or lead bath.

**Castellate:** To form metal into a castellated shape such as castellated nut, etc.

**Chamfer:** To bevel a sharp corner or edge.

**Chase:** A term describing the cutting of threads in a lathe, as distinguished from cutting with a die.

**Chill:** Hardening the surface of cast iron by chilling in a metal mold.

**Color-Harden:** Case hardening to shallow depth, done for mottled appearance.

**Core:** In foundry practice, to form the hollow part of a casting.

**Counterbore:** A cylindrical enlargement of the end of a cylinder bore. A tool with a piloted end used for this purpose.

**Countersink:** To drill or otherwise form a depression of a given depth to take the conical head of a screw flush with the surrounding surface. The tool used for this purpose.

**Crown:** An angular contour, higher at the center, as the face of a flat-belt pulley.

**Die:** (a) A formed and hardened metal block for shaping or impressing a design into sheet metal or cutting a shaped disk or other form from sheet metal.
(b) A tool for cutting external threads.

**Die Casting:** An accurate, smooth casting resulting from pressing or forcing a molten alloy under pressure into metal mold.

**Die Stamping:** The sheet metal object shaped or cut by a die.

**Draw:** (a) To elongate or form by a distorting operation or process.
(b) To temper steel by quenching at timed intervals.

**Drill:** To sink a hole into or through a piece of metal, usually with a twist drill.

**Drop Forging:** A piece of wrought metal formed hot to desired shape with dies, either by pressure or under a forging or drop hammer.

**Face:** To true a flat surface in a lathe, the surface being perpendicular to the axis of rotation.

**File:** To remove metal from the surface with a file.

**Fillet:** A rounded filling of the corner formed by two parts meeting or joined at an angle.

**Fin:** A thin rib projecting from the main body, as on an air-cooled cylinder.

**Fit:** The contact, or perhaps more properly, the interference between two machined surfaces and generally described as "drive," "force," or "press" fit,—"shrink," where heat is used to expand one of the parts,—"running" or "sliding," where free movement of a shaft must be allowed, and "wringing," where interference of the shaft is greater than the running or sliding fit and one part must be twisted, by hand, into the other.

**Flange:** A projecting rim for stiffening, fastening, or limiting movement.

**Forge:** To shape hot metal, either by hammering or by a pressure process.

**Graduate:** To indicate a division of a scale or instrument dial or other measuring device into regular or uniform spaces.

**Grinding:** The process of finishing a surface with a grinding wheel or disk.

**Key:** A small piece of metal inserted in an opening which is generally cut half in the shaft and half in the hub of a wheel or gear to prevent movement of the parts one over the other.

**Keyway:** A groove or slot cut to take a key of given size.

**Knurling:** The process of uniformly indenting a turned part or surface to give a surer hand or finger grip.

**Lap:** A piece of metal, wood, leather, or rubber charged with fine abrasive and used for the purpose of imparting an accurate finish. To finish by lapping.

# of Shop Terms

**Lug:** A projecting part of a casting or forging generally rectangular in section or shape, differing in this respect from a boss.

**Malleable Casting:** A small casting to which a degree of toughness is imparted by a process of annealing.

**Mill:** To machine true surfaces, grooves, and the like with a rotating cutter.

**Pack Hardening:** A process which, in a sense, combines the two processes of carburizing and case hardening.

**Pad:** A shallow projection usually formed on a casting for the purpose of mounting some separate part to be attached with bolts or screws. Differs from a boss in shape and size.

**Peen:** The act of stretching or distorting metal by strokes of a ball-peen hammer. Applies to hand riveting and art metal work.

**Pickling:** A process of cleaning castings in hot bath of weak sulphuric acid solution.

**Plane:** To finish work on a planer, a machine having a fixed cutting tool and moving table or bed.

**Planishing:** A process of finishing sheet metal by hammering with hammers having polished faces.

**Polishing:** A frictional process with a fine abrasive or rouge to impart a lustrous finish.

**Profiling:** Machining an outline or contour with a rotary cutter, the movement of which is controlled by a master die or shape exactly the same of that of the outline.

**Punch:** Usually applies to perforating sheet metal of varying thicknesses with a non-rotating tool.

**Ream:** To bring a drilled hole to accurate diameter with a rotating fluted tool.

**Relief:** Variations in the plane surfaces of two or more parts in an assembly or in the machined or formed surfaces of a single piece. Briefly, one plane surface above or below another.

**Riveting:** Peening or upsetting the protruding end of a rivet or pin which is used to fasten two or more parts permanently together.

**Sandblasting:** To clean rough castings or forgings with sharp sand driven through a nozzle by compressed air.

**Shape:** To shape metal on a shaper, the latter a machine tool differing from the planer in that the tool moves and the work is held stationary.

**Shear:** To cut sheet metal or brass in a machine having two blades.

**Shim:** A spacer of thin sheet metal used for adjusting clearances in bearings, blocking an object at proper height, position, etc.

**Spin:** To shape a piece of rotating sheet metal in a lathe by forcing it, with special tools, to take shape against a form.

**Spline:** A long keyway or series of keyways cut about the circumference of a shaft,—as a splined end.

**Spot Face:** To finish a circular spot on a rough or irregular surface with an end milling cutter for the purpose of seating a capscrew or bolt head.

**Spot Weld:** To weld in a series of spots by heat resistance to electric current, applicable to all except sheet copper and brass.

**Steel Casting:** Ordinary cast iron alloyed with varying amounts of scrap steel.

**Swage:** To shape metal by hammering or by pressure over a swage block.

**Sweat:** To join metal by sweat soldering wherein two pieces are clamped together with solder between and heat applied until the solder melts and flows.

**Tack Weld:** To join parts by a series of short welds.

**Tap:** To cut threads in a drilled hole with a tap.

**Temper:** To change the physical characteristics of steel by heat treating.

**Template:** A pattern for laying out or transferring shapes, the location of a series of holes, etc.

**Tolerance:** The total of the acceptable variations in the size of a machined part.

**Tumble:** To clean and smooth rough castings, forgings, or other parts by placing them in a rotating drum and adding such mediums as metal scraps, hardened balls, etc.

**Turn:** To machine work in a lathe, commonly taken to mean parts mounted between centers. Differs from facing.

**Upset:** To forge, by means of hammering or pressure, a section of larger diameter on a bar.

**Welding:** Primarily taken to mean the joining of two pieces by heating to the fusing point and pressing or hammering together.

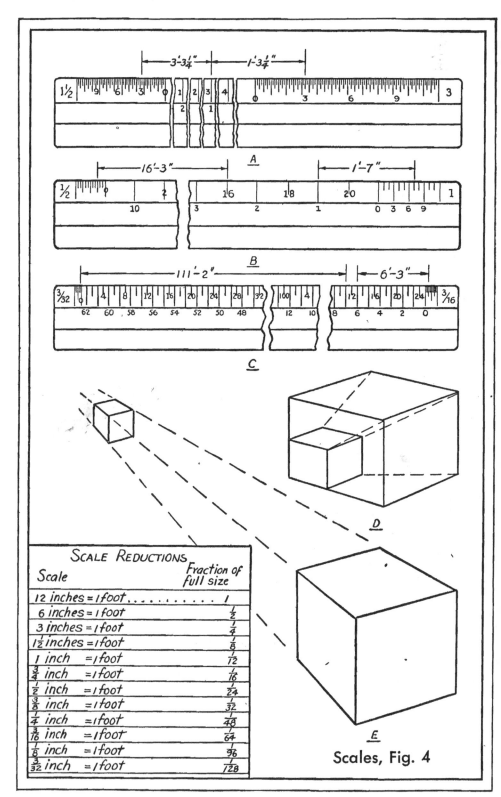

Scales, Fig. 4

| SCALE REDUCTIONS | |
|---|---|
| Scale | Fraction of full size |
| 12 inches = 1 foot . . . . . . . . . . | 1 |
| 6 inches = 1 foot | $\frac{1}{2}$ |
| 3 inches = 1 foot | $\frac{1}{4}$ |
| 1½ inches = 1 foot | $\frac{1}{8}$ |
| 1 inch = 1 foot | $\frac{1}{12}$ |
| $\frac{3}{4}$ inch = 1 foot | $\frac{1}{16}$ |
| $\frac{1}{2}$ inch = 1 foot | $\frac{1}{24}$ |
| $\frac{3}{8}$ inch = 1 foot | $\frac{1}{32}$ |
| $\frac{1}{4}$ inch = 1 foot | $\frac{1}{48}$ |
| $\frac{3}{16}$ inch = 1 foot | $\frac{1}{64}$ |
| $\frac{1}{8}$ inch = 1 foot | $\frac{1}{96}$ |
| $\frac{3}{32}$ inch = 1 foot | $\frac{1}{128}$ |

might be termed "pictorial" values as well, that is, they make it possible for the draftsman to show certain assemblies of parts more nearly as a picture and as such are a definite aid to clarity and ease of interpretation. The cross-hatching indicating either one or several materials of parts in partial or complete assembly or adjacent to one another not only designates the material but defines the separate parts more clearly.

## Scales:

Obviously, large objects cannot be conveniently detailed full size. The outlines and other parts must be uniformly reduced in size on the drawing so that the sheets will be easy to handle and examine and also of a standard or uniform size so that they may be filed conveniently. Hence, drawings are nearly always made to a reduced scale, that is, every part is drawn to a predetermined fraction of the full size. However, there are certain comparatively rare instances where an enlarged scale must be used. In such cases a notation on the drawing will state that the details are twice actual size, three times actual size, and so on. Continuing to consider scale reductions in size, once the draftsman has decided on a given scale reduction, such as ¾ in. equals 1 foot, he must be careful to determine beforehand whether this scale is practical, that is, that this particular scale will not reduce some parts to such small size that they are difficult to draw and to show clearly. A scale reduction within practical limits must be calculated for the smallest detailed part of the whole unit if it is of involved construction. To make this easy the draftsman uses a scale, Fig. 4, which may be a single triangular-shaped unit or a set of several scales which are like small rulers except that the edges are beveled and are graduated into various scale reductions. What the scale actually does is indicate given distances representing one foot. Then this given distance is subdivided into 12 parts by graduations, each graduation representing one inch. Then the twelfths are again subdivided into halves and quarters representing ½ and ¼ of an inch. Now looking at detail A in Fig. 4 and reading first from right to left, you notice the figure 1½ at the extreme left. This means that this portion of the scale is sub-

divided in a scale reduction of 1½ inches equals 1 foot or in reality ⅛ of a foot actual foot-rule measurement, as you see by the table below. Taking a measurement from the object to be drawn, let us say, the draftsman finds that a scale reduction of 1½ inches equals 1 foot will serve the purpose of convenience. One particular part of the object he finds is 3 feet 3¼ inches long by actual measurement. He must reduce this to exact scale along with all other parts. So he looks to the right of the "O"-line on the 1½ inch division of the scale until he finds the figure 3. Then to the left of the O-line he counts three 1-inch divisions or three of those divisions representing twelfths. These are subdivided into fourths so he adds one of the fourths and this completes the reading, 3 feet 3¼ inches.

Then in detail B, Fig. 4, you see scale reductions of ½ inch equals 1 foot and 1 inch equals 1 foot. You will notice, too, that on these scales some of the graduations have been omitted for the purpose of clarity. In detail C are scales representing just about the smallest practical reductions of the standard foot measurement and fractions thereof. These reductions are used where the object or machine to be detailed is of large size with no very small parts which, in the same scale, would reduce to a size impractical to draw and dimension. In extreme cases the draftsman sometimes separates these parts and shows them in a lesser reduction and so notes the fact on the drawing so that there will be no error. Heretofore on those scales shown in Fig. 4, the reductions show 12 divisions but if you note carefully the ³⁄₃₂-inch reduction, detail C, shows only 6 divisions which means that each division represents 2 inches. The same is true of the ⅛-inch reduction. Any further graduation of these reductions would make the divisions virtually invisible, hence of no practical value. The scale then is simply a reduced foot rule for laying off and determining the measurement and consequently the size of the drawing which represents the machine and its parts all reduced uniformly. The thing to keep in mind is that the dimension on the drawing is the actual measurement of the part in feet and inches or fractions of an inch. In other words the dimensions are those of the object itself, but if you measured the distance on the drawing in feet and inches, with a common foot rule, you would find it considerably less because the distance or dimension has been reduced by means of the scale, or reduced foot rule. Sketches D and E may help in visualizing the reductions more clearly. One has to think of the object itself made uniformly smaller by the scale reductions, like the same object viewed at a distance as at E.

Going farther into scale reduction of parts, many drafting rooms are now supplied with a standard-sized sheet which includes a title box. In this are spaces for the common filing and record data, material specifications, and any other instructions or information pertinent to the particular drawing included. In addition, the designing and engineering staffs often arrange a schedule of standard tolerances made applicable to a given machine design or type or a series of parts of a machine. This data is printed on the sheets and serves as a guide to both the draftsman and the machinist. On these sheets, which are comparatively small for convenience in handling and filing, it is becoming a common practice to detail only one or two parts. Each sheet usually carries a key number and the name of the part. By this procedure the chance of error is greatly minimized. There is a considerable saving in time both in the drafting room and the machine shop for the prints are easier to read and work from.

The scale rules with which the draftsman lays off the scale reductions are of two general types. One, Fig. 4, A, B, and C, comes as a set of several scales shaped much like ordinary 1-ft. rulers except that generally the four corners are beveled and all these bevels usually carry scale reductions. The other type is a triangular-shaped rule 1 ft. long with a 1 ft graduation in inches on one bevel. Other beveled faces are graduated in the common scale reductions.

**Simple Views:**

Up to now we've been talking about lines, the fundamentals of the various combinations in which they are used and the specific purpose of each one, that is, what the draftsman and blueprint reader must know about lines and the terms describing directly or indirectly their various

uses, and symbolic meanings. Now to see how the draftsman and blueprint reader put this information to practical use. Taking a look first at Fig. 5, A, the angular arrangement of lines here defines the outlines of a rectangular object which may be anything, a box for example, and if we assume that it is a box then it must be kept in mind that only the outlines are shown, that is, the lines defining the outermost limits of what we can see, the side, top, and end. Hence ,the view of the box is not fully detailed for if it were, we would see the visible ends of the side pieces and also the top and bottom pieces where these over-lap the edges of the end piece. And inasmuch as there are no dotted lines indicating irregularity in the invisible outline we can assume that the top and bottom, and the two ends and sides, are duplicates. So for the purpose of identification we can call this a perspective view, although the perspective is not entirely true. In other words, what we actually have is an isometric view of the box. Certain elongations of the lines which would give the required fore-shortening have been omitted for the purpose of clarity and ease of sketching. As it stands, the box could be dimensioned over-all by simply giving the width, length and depth, the latter in this case referring to the distance from the top to bottom.

But if more details are to be dimensioned such as the thickness of the sides, ends, bottom and top, then the extension and dimension lines tend to become confusing, that is, they are in "each other's way," so to speak. Some dimension lines would have to be set off on unduly long extension lines. Others might have to be so placed that the lines would cross. This is not an approved practice, of course, although it is sometimes permissible when time is pressing or when designing and machining departments are working in close touch.

So in making up mechanical drawings it is generally assumed that the size of the parts or part is a primary consideration, that is, when there is any question about how to detail a part or parts of any mechanism the prominent display and arrangement of the dimension lines usually comes first and may even, in certain cases, cause the draftsman to make some change in what otherwise would be a characteristic.

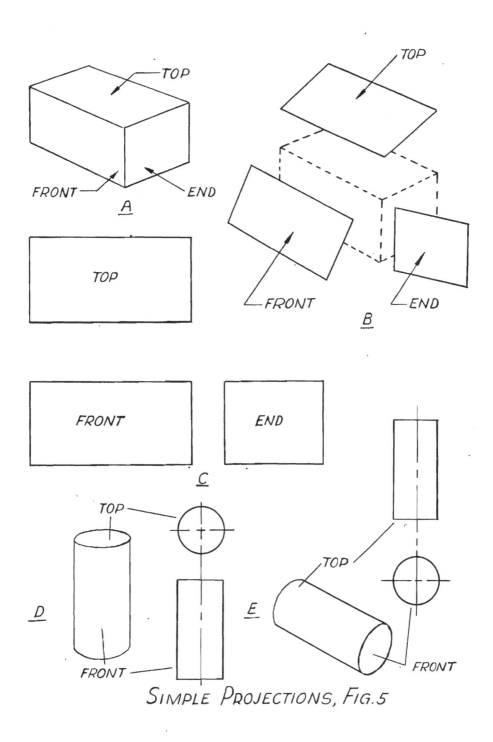

SIMPLE PROJECTIONS, FIG. 5

presentation of the object in its several parts. In other words, dimension lines must not be placed so that their reading will tend to be obscure or confusing.

So as a standard practice which has been found effective for the greatest number of variations in drawings the draftsman would give a top, side, and end view of the box as at C, Fig. 5. To make it more clear just what he does, Fig. 5, B, shows how he figuratively lifts off the top, one side, and one end of the box and makes a separate drawing of each. Usually drawings of more simple objects are arranged as in Fig. 5, C, but when necessary to show a bottom view or some other detail, the views are arranged differently, the exact placing determined by the nature of the subject. The three simple views shown in Fig. 5, C, are an example of what is known as "third-angle" or orthographic projection.

Of course, one should avoid confusion by keeping in mind that not every subject is so projected. Only those, like the box, which require three or more views are thus presented. Fig. 5, D and E, are examples of where only two views are necessary in ordinary work. Both show essentially the same object. Here the cylindrical object has no detail characteristics other than the fact that it is of the same diameter throughout the length. The ends are square. As they stand, these two objects, for purposes of measurement alone, have only two dimensions, diameter and length. So all that is necessary in this instance is a down, or plan view, and a side view. On drawings of such cylindrical objects, side view is merely a term of "convenience," as it were. It is accepted as such simply because no matter which way you turned the cylinder the same contour would be presented.

Having come thus far, one can conclude that in order to build solely from them, it is very necessary to have drawings from which dimensions may be taken. It is very essential that these drawings show and dimension every constructional detail, and at the same time they must enable the reader to visualize the object to be constructed in part and in entirety. In order to build anything it is necessary to know what it looks like.

It is just as necessary for the blueprint reader to make some study of the manner in which we observe things. The whole thing resolves itself into how information as to size, shape, and dimension of an object may be recorded and transmitted intelligibly to the machinist, and how he in turn may visualize first and then translate into action, which usually means machine setups, the information which appears on the blueprint.

Now, how can the prospective blueprint reader make at least an elemental study of how mechanical objects really look? First of all, one must "adjust" his mind. And then the eye must be trained to see just the things you're looking for. Go back to the drawing of the box, A, in Fig. 5, or set a small box directly in front of you when seated at a table, so that the outlines of the box approximate those shown at A, or in other words, have the box in the same relative position. You see the top, side, and end. Now, move it just a trifle. If you observe closely, you will note that all those outlines you can see have changed position just slightly. The same box in essentially the same position, but you have a different view. Then you will note that by moving the box only slightly you can get any number of views of it. To continue farther with this simple little experiment, raise the box to exact eye level and hold it so that the side is at right angles to your point of view. Now you see the side only, nothing more. In fact, the side, from your point of view, is no longer even identified with the box. You can feel the shape and outline of the box but you cannot see it. The side is simply a flat or plane surface having a top and bottom and end outline but to your eye it has no thickness, that is, depth. In other words the third dimension is unseen. And if you tip the box so that the top is toward you, the same thing happens. Only the plane surface of the top can be seen. Now turn the box through a 45-degree angle so that you see only the end. Again the same condition holds.

What you have actually done is project the outlines of the box into three separate views, each one of them representing the same thing you saw when looking directly at the top, side, and end respectively while the box was held at eye level. Of course, one should keep in mind that the box could hardly be termed a part of any mechanical device. It is serving merely as a means of illustration.

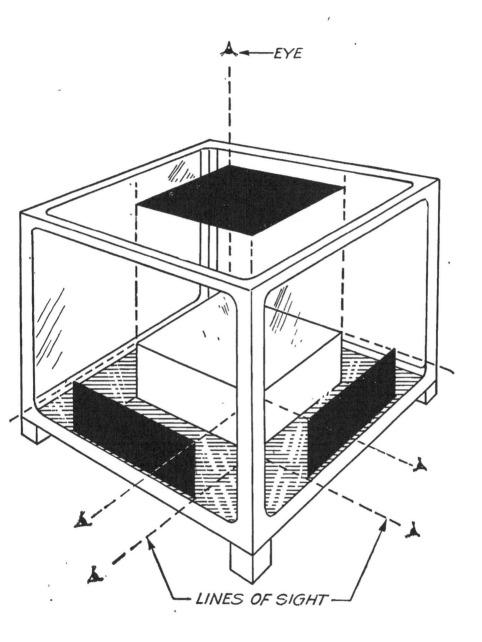

*Fig.5A, Projection of Views To Sides of Showcase*

## Show Case Presentation:

Now, going a bit farther and getting at the point in a rather different, and to some, perhaps a clearer way. Think of a glass showcase, approximately square, with the box inside it, as in Fig. 5A. Now, using your imagination further, suppose that you stand over the case and sight down the four corners of the box from a point directly above each corner as indicated. Mark these four points where the line of sight passes through the glass. Then cut a piece of black paper to such size that the four corners come exactly on the four points marked on the glass. Suppose, then, that the paper is pasted to the glass making a black square as indicated. Still using the imagination, suppose that you proceed in exactly the same way with the side and right-hand end of the box. Then you will have what you see in Fig. 5A. Using the imagination still further, suppose that the top and right-hand side of the showcase were hinged at the front so that you could raise the top to a vertical position and swing the right-hand end outward until it is in line with the front. And there you are, with three views of the box, a projected top, side, and end view, all lying in the same plane. Compare with details B and C in Fig. 5, and the point will be clear. Projecting views of an object in this third-angle fashion is just what the draftsman does with any object, the complete dimensioning of which requires three or more views. It is essential that the student of blueprint reading get this method clearly in mind. And it should be remembered, too, that the box which has been used thus far only serves as a simple object to illustrate the principle. Later on we'll see how a simple machine part is projected in the same way as were the three views of the box. The machine part will bear very little if any resemblance to the box but you'll recognize the method at once, if you've made a careful study of the fundamental idea and purpose.

## Irregular Shapes:

Now something rather different. Fig. 6 shows three views of what basically is the same object, except that in the second and third views an extra detail or two has been added. Note carefully how the projected views record the addition of these details.

The third part, C, is basically the same as the first, A, yet in detail it is a much more complicated affair as you will see at a glance. For convenience we can think of the object shown as a small block of steel and of the various surface details, grooves and step cuts, as having been cut or milled on a milling machine. It should be understood, of course, that should the specifications call for the block to be finished in the machine shop to the shape shown in Fig. 6 C, then details A and B would not be given on the blueprint. Only the shape C with all dimensions, notes, and other necessary data would be detailed and this would be used by the machinist in making the part. In all these drawings or projections of the object, notice particularly how the top side, and end views include all surface details in such a way that they can be dimensioned without extending the dimension or extension lines over or across one another and the dimension figures will not be so closely grouped as to make them difficult to read or confused as to meaning. The second view and detail drawing includes a characteristic (groove) which in one view is invisible and is indicated by a dotted line. Even though only this one view were shown you would know from the characteristics and position of the dotted line that this particular detail is invisible, yet you would have no dimension of it. From this perhaps we can see more clearly why it is necessary for the draftsman to project the detail drawings of such an object into the three views we've been talking about. Where no isometric or perspective drawing is included, as is done in Fig. 6, it is essential that such an object as that shown be detailed with three views, otherwise the blueprint reader would have little idea of what the part really looked like and also it would be difficult to visualize it as to size. The third drawing and perspective view serves further to emphasize this point. Here a hidden detail appears in each view as the subject is further complicated in outline by grooves. No one or even two views would detail the object fully but three views show every characteristic necessary to complete dimensioning.

## Arrangement of Four Views:

Going a step farther, Fig. 6A shows one method the draftsman uses in presenting

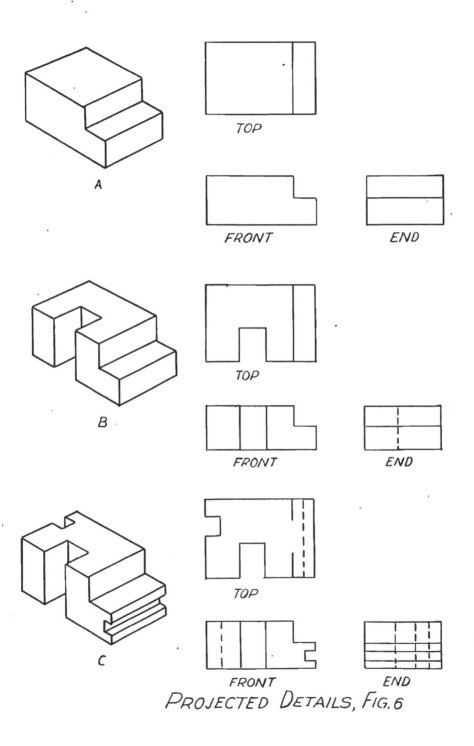

TOP

FRONT

END

A

TOP

FRONT

END

B

TOP

FRONT

END

C

PROJECTED DETAILS, FIG. 6

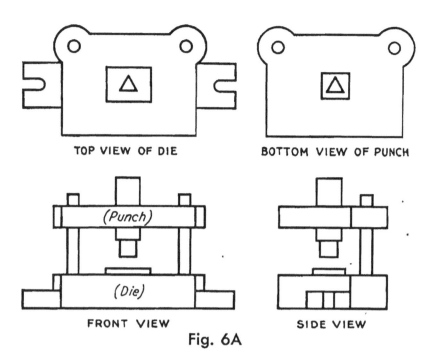

TOP VIEW OF DIE          BOTTOM VIEW OF PUNCH

(Punch)

(Die)

FRONT VIEW          SIDE VIEW

Fig. 6A

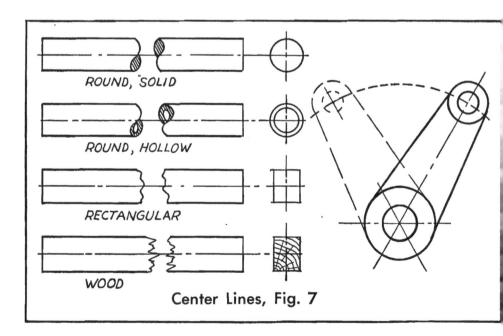

ROUND, SOLID

ROUND, HOLLOW

RECTANGULAR

WOOD          Center Lines, Fig. 7

and arranging the drawings of an object requiring four views. Another arrangement of views of the same subject would be placing the top, front, and bottom view on a vertical centerline with the side view located to the right of the front view, although on some drawings the side view can be placed directly to the right of the top view. The arrangement is largely dictated by the nature and character of the object and the necessary views are so drawn and arranged as to best describe its shape. The four views in Fig. 6A are simple outline drawings as you will see, for no centerlines, dotted lines indicating invisible details, or dimension lines are shown. Notice, too, that these views are carefully and explicitly titled so that there will be no mistake in the reading. It should be understood that the bottom view is a view "looking up" and is used when operations or characteristics are best shown when looking directly at the bottom of the part. In this particular instance, Fig. 6A, the drawing of the bottom of the punch is placed to the right, in line with the top view of the die just as if it were turned over from the top view. One exception in connection with bottom views: These are not used in steel plate and structural drawings. Instead, the view is usually shown as a sectional view looking down, the cutting plane generally passing a little above the bottom.

## Center Lines:

A center line is really what might be called a "convenience" line. It serves as a locating line and as a base line and also as a reference line drawn by the draftsman to aid in making a drawing, when such center lines as are required are first drawn and then the various views are made by laying off dimensions from those lines. They also have what one might term "pictorial" value; they "finish" a drawing, lead the eye naturally from one view to another, they connect views, indicate definite relationships of one part to another. Visualize, for example, how the views in Fig. 7 would be changed if the center lines were omitted. One cardinal rule to remember: A center line is never used as a dimension line, according to standard established practice. Particularly, center lines are essential when the details have been located,

but have not been fully drawn, where necessary measurements are to be laid off from the center line, and especially where parts to be built must be laid out directly from the drawing. Sometimes the working drawing must be traced or transferred to the surface of the material from which the part or parts are to be cut. Then the center lines are of first importance as they must be considered by the workman first of all.

## Eye Level View of Circular Object:

If you hold any hollow circular object endwise at eye level you can look through it as well as at it. As an example, if you take a short length cut from a piece of cardboard tubing and hold it with its horizontal center line at eye level so that its end lies in a plane at right angles to your line of sight, you see not only the forward end, (the end nearest you), but a portion of the inside of the rim as well. In other words you really see the depth, that is, you are aware of it by sight alone. In this way it differs from the side of the box held in the same position. Still holding the same object at eye level, rotate it slightly to the right and you get something like the effect shown in the upper left-hand detail, Fig. 7A. Rotate it farther to the left as shown in the right-hand detail and you will note that you see a portion of the outer face of the rim while a corresponding portion of the inner surface of the rim disappears from view. From this simple little experiment one can easily see what a difficult time the draftsman would have if he attempted to detail pulleys, wheels, gears, and the like, in perspective views either at or below eye level. So to avoid the difficulty of dimensioning such an object and also to save himself a lot of time and trouble in making the drawing, the draftsman generally represents such objects with a simple side view such as the lower view in Fig. 7A. Here the characteristics of the rim, such as the crown, inside taper or bevel of the rim to the parting line and the thickness at the edge of the rim, are shown by spaced concentric circles as you see. These are either complete circles or segments with the ends connected to the curves or fillets on either side of the spokes, or more properly, when referring to pulleys or gears, arms. Later on we will see

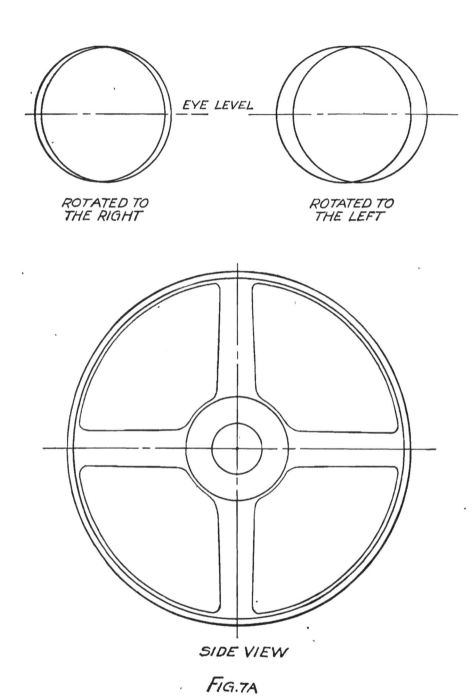

EYE LEVEL

ROTATED TO
THE RIGHT

ROTATED TO
THE LEFT

SIDE VIEW

FIG. 7A

ow the draftsman completes such a drawing by adding a sectional view.

## elation of Objects to echanical Drawings:

It's an old axiom that "you learn to do y doing" and to paraphrase it, "you learn see by seeing." Ordinarily one "sees" e instant he opens his eyes and we can e many objects in a room and identify em simply by name. Objects' about the me which have long since become familiar we do not identify by name unless e have to refer them to someone else. In her words, we see them in only one way, d we think of them in only one way. But ppose for example that imaginary circumstances made it necessary to make mplete constructional (working) drawgs of, for instance, our bookcase—for me friend in a distant city who desires make a duplicate of it, let us say. Now, e bookcase takes on an entirely new significance. It is no longer just a bookcase. 7e must look at it in an entirely different ay and we have to think of it in an enrely different way. We must think of it ither as a composite of all its parts, where ach of those parts fits, what relation it ears to another and to the whole. We ust know the exact size of every part, very joint, every screw, and we must ow solely by means of drawings exactly e dimensions of every part and we must dicate precisely where it goes. In other ords, we must have a clear mental picre of the bookcase assembly, its size, and ow it is put together. We can no longer ink of it and visualize it just as a conenient place to store books. And if we iscipline both mind and eye .we can see ese relationships in almost any object. stead of being an assembly of wheels, ears, bearings, shafts, and castings, the ookcase is merely a structure whose parts re of both wood and metal made in a furiture or woodworking shop, instead of a undry and machine shop. Yet both the achine and the bookcase bear essentially e same relation to the drawings which ere made in designing and drafting rooms efore the two were built in the shops. omeone had to visualize pleasing, praccal, and workable and usable objects, omeone had to draw the constructional etails of the parts and dimension them

and then someone had to take these drawings and from them make the parts and assemble them into the finished units. From this you can see that even many of the familiar objects about your home may have all their constructional and assembly characteristics recorded in accurate measured drawings and from these any experienced craftsman could duplicate the object in every detail even though he had never seen the original. And remember, too, that these would be scale drawings with perhaps only a few small parts or assemblies shown full-size.. Now to change our thinking to subjects of a mechanical nature, Fig. 8 shows perspective views and accompanying mechanical drawings of several objects more or less familiar to every machinist. All of them are actual machine parts or accessory tools and fittings. Here we see first of all additional features in shape easily seen in the perspective views. The important thing is to note how the accompanying mechanical drawings record these variations. Take the first one, A, for example. This one introduces a new shape, a dowel, peg, or pilot projecting from the main cylindrical body. If we take away the perspective view entirely we still will know that the object portrayed by the line arrangement in the mechanical drawing is cylindrical in shape and has two diameters. Now, one important point to note carefully: Disregarding the perspective view, we know from the plan view that the object is cylindrical, that in fact there are two cylindrical sections, and from this we also know the object is represented as though we were looking down on its top from a point directly above it, that is, our line of sight coincides with the center line of the object itself. Figuratively speaking, if we move the eye in any direction from this point, we will see something else. Refer to the top views in Fig. 7A again. This plan view is a view "looking down" from a vertical viewpoint instead of "looking at" the object from a horizontal viewpoint at eye level. The latter, or front view, is often referred to as an "elevation" although this term is not so frequently used now in referring to drawings of mechanical objects. The two circles, full lines, in the top or plan view, Fig. 8, A, represent first, the outside edge of the cylinder, and second, the outside edge of the smaller projection,

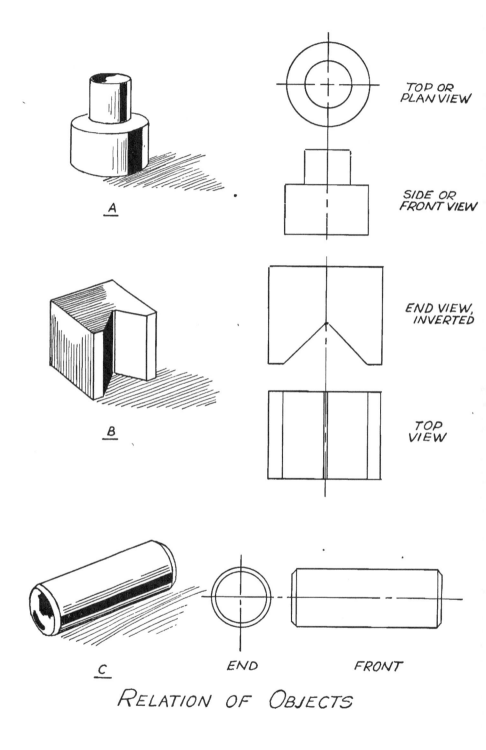

A

TOP OR
PLAN VIEW

SIDE OR
FRONT VIEW

B

END VIEW,
INVERTED

TOP
VIEW

C

END

FRONT

RELATION OF OBJECTS

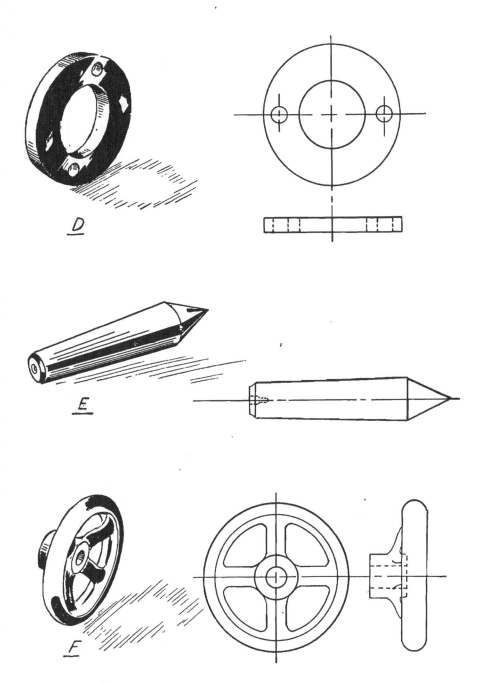

D

E

F

*To the Mechanical Drawing, Fig.8*

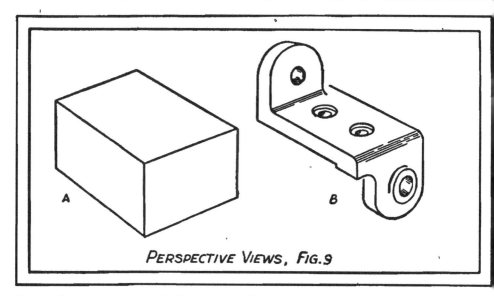

PERSPECTIVE VIEWS, FIG.9

that is, the two concentric full circles are made to serve this purpose. Again in the elevation or front view we are looking directly at the object from the front as if it were held at a comfortable distance in front of us with the center at eye level.

Fig. 8, B, shows the same combination of perspective view and mechanical drawing. This time the object is a V-block, a familiar tool around the drillpress and at the machinist's bench for use in holding round work on a surface plate, etc. It is usually milled from tool steel with parallel flat surfaces and with Vees milled into one or more of the faces as shown. Notice again how the simple drawings record the surface characteristics of the part. The whole drawing is merely a symmetrical arrangement of straight solid lines joined at square and angle corners. Now, the drawing at C presents what one might first think a contradiction of the rule that all unseen edges in drawings are represented by dotted lines. In this, reference is made to the chamfer at the ends of the steel pin represented by the lines drawn at an angle of 45° (the usual angle of a chamfer, although there are exceptions). The reason for the common practice of not showing dotted lines here is that usually the draftsman designates this particular operation as "Chamfer 45°" or "Chamfer ⅟₁₆"," the latter dimension usually referring to the distance between the angle corners of the chamfer cut and as the extension lines are

generally perpendicular to the axis, the dimension does not generally refer to the actual width of the chamfer as measured across its face.

The drawings for the retainer ring show hidden details. Very often on such a piece of work the degree of finish and the diameters (inner and outer) are given in notes in place of the common dimension lines. The same thing is frequently true of the pin in Fig. 8, C. Usually such a pin is either of cold-rolled steel for ordinary purposes, such as a dowel or guide pin, or it may be of special analysis steel which is carburized, heat-treated, or otherwise hardened to such a degree that it can be ground to dimensions within critical limits. The chamfers at the ends are for the purpose of making it easy to start the pin in the holes into which it may be an easy fit or in the case of higher class work, a "wringing" or drive fit. In some cases such pins are a "shrink" fit in one part and a free fit in another which means usually that half the pin is anchored by heating the adjacent area in one part and shrinking onto the pin. Then the projecting end of the pin enters a registering hole in a second part. In such assemblies it is referred to as a dowel, guide, or locating pin. The washer-like ring is frequently used as a retainer ring in certain types of bearing assemblies and as such often requires a critical finish.

The drawing for the lathe center, E, is

not complete. Usually, not always, the sizes and finishing details will be given as notes. Generally the taper, for example, is not dimensioned but is specified as "No. 1 Morse taper," "No. 2 Morse taper," and so on. The drawing would give the number of the countersink to be used in the small end and, if standard, the general specifications would designate a 60-degree lathe center and would state whether for head stock or tail stock. In the latter case the center would be hardened.

The two mechanical drawings of the hand wheel, Fig. 8, F, show hidden details which are outlines. In this drawing contours turn up for the first time. Looking only at the side or front view of the wheel you would not know, unless you were familiar with this particular wheel, the exact shape of the rim section. It might be square or rectangular in section (looking at it edgewise) or it might even be round or nearly so. In addition we would not know about the angular offset of the arms. However, the edgewise view, looking at the rim edgewise, gives one this information about the shape of these details. Ordinarily, the rim would not be shown full on a working drawing but rather as a sectional view of which we will learn more later. Now, the important point in the relation of the drawing to the object: In Fig. 8 we see only one-part objects of comparatively simple outline. But suppose certain of these, such as the pin, retainer, lathe center, or hand wheel, represented only one part of a machine consisting of many, perhaps even hundreds, of parts detailed on a set of blueprints. Then it would be necessary for the one reading the blueprints to study the characteristics of each part separately in order to familiarize oneself with the assembly to such an extent that the entire machine could be visualized. As has been remarked before, the simple practice of studying various objects for the sole purpose of correlating the object with a mechanical drawing made of it, is a very valuable help. And it is essential that one learn to think of how the subject of study will look on the blueprint, not just how it appears to the eye. This study is just the reverse of a study of the blueprint without the subject to look at. Here in the latter case, one has to visualize the appearance and constructional details of the completed

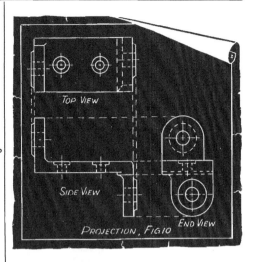

project. In the former instance, one must think of how the subject will look in a mechanical drawing.

Another excellent practice is to actually make mechanical drawings, starting with simple objects, of course. Unless one has had some training in mechanical drawing, he will likely be very much discouraged at the outset, but if one persists, he will soon find that it is not at all difficult to make a practical working drawing of almost any simple subject of a constructional nature.

No need to possess an elaborate set of drawing instruments, T-squares, triangles, tables, and the like, at the start. Just a ruler, a pencil, a sheet of paper and a few simple points clearly in mind: Keep the various views of the object in the correct position relative to each other. Show all hidden parts with the correct dotted lines. Outlines of round objects appear as straight lines when one looks at them edgewise at eye level and that's the way one is to show them on the drawing. The top and bottom end of a round paper carton, a piece of pipe, or a can, appear on the drawing as straight lines, in fact any front view of a cylindrical object is made to appear as a square or rectangle, depending on its length of course, when one looks directly at it. Furthermore, at the beginning, one will perhaps get a more practical and personal contact with a drawing by copying from an original. In this work one will of necessity have to duplicate the work of the draftsman in making that particular drawing, not as skillfully perhaps at the start,

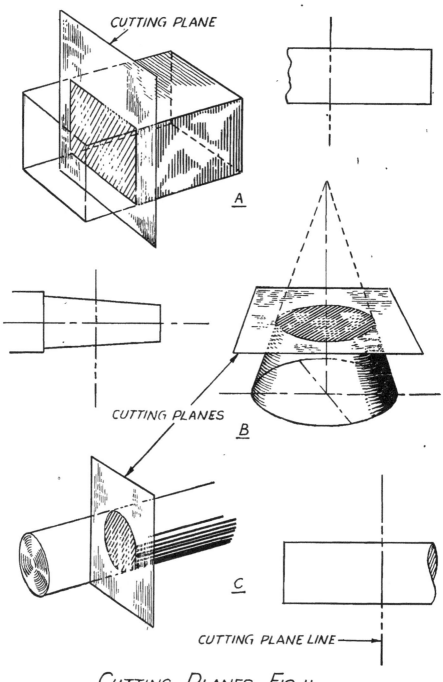

CUTTING PLANE

*A*

CUTTING PLANES

*B*

CUTTING PLANES

*C*

CUTTING PLANE LINE ⟶

CUTTING PLANES, FIG. 11

but from persistent effort one will acquire a practical knowledge of the draftsman's technique. Training in manual skill is only a question of practice. Anyone contemplating entering the machine trades will do well to have a practical working knowledge of at least the rudimentary principles of mechanical drawing. It is a most valuable help in reading advanced blueprints.

**Perspective Views:**

Fig. 9 turns up two perspective views, one of the now familiar box, A, the other

part is to be cast, but more likely, so represented, it is a metal part on which all machining operations have been performed. In other words, the view represents the part as it appears when finished. That conclusion reached, there are several things we can determine with a fair chance of accuracy just at a glance. We know that it is undoubtedly some special form of bracket with two projections or "lips" which are slightly off-center. On the front lip, the one nearest us, projecting downward, we see an integral raised projection

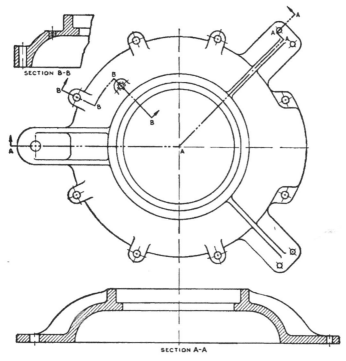

## Fig. 11A

of a machine part, B, presenting several more advanced design details. Both are placed side by side purposely so that the student will again see the basic analogy of the two views. Now as an example, let's assume that we are presented with the drawing, B, just as it stands. It has no title, no dimensions, no indication of the character of hidden details. We do not have any idea of precisely what it is or what it is for, as we have never seen the part, nor has it been described to us. It may represent a pattern of wood from which a metal

or "boss," (refer to Shop Terms) which is usually cast integral so that it may be machined true for the purpose of seating a machine screw or machine bolt. We can assume that there is also a boss in the same relative position on the back (invisible) face of the left-hand lip. However, we do not know for certain. Noting that the two holes which appear in line through the horizontal section are countersunk we can conclude that the nature of the assembly of which this bracket is a part requires that the bolt or machine-screw heads be flush

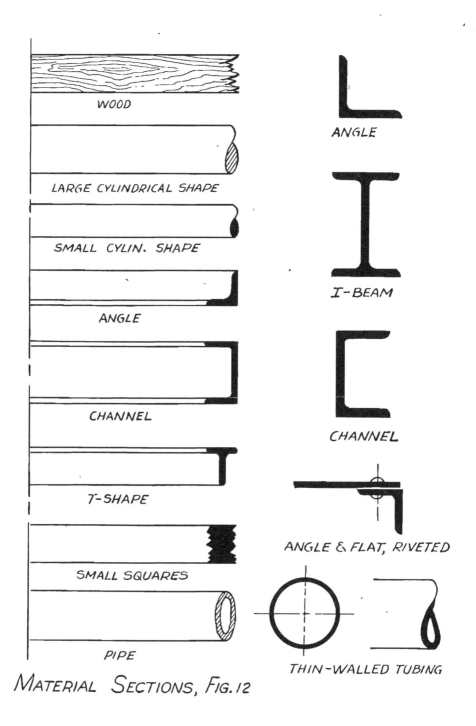

WOOD

LARGE CYLINDRICAL SHAPE

SMALL CYLIN. SHAPE

ANGLE

CHANNEL

T-SHAPE

SMALL SQUARES

PIPE

ANGLE

I-BEAM

CHANNEL

ANGLE & FLAT, RIVETED

THIN-WALLED TUBING

MATERIAL SECTIONS, FIG. 12

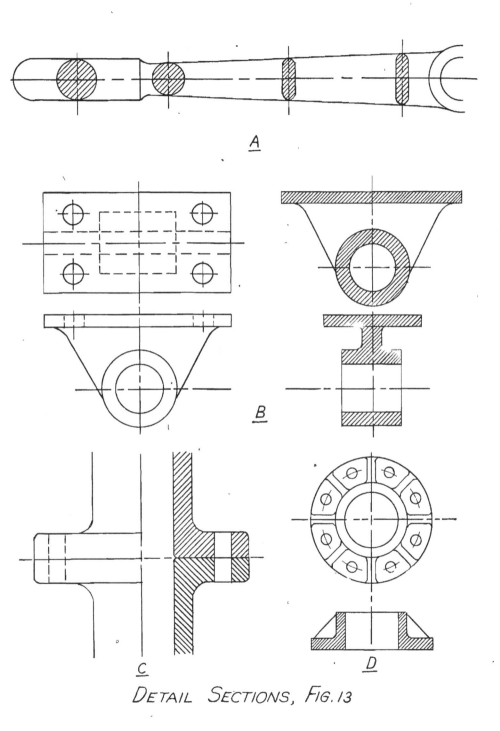

DETAIL SECTIONS, FIG. 13

with or slightly below the surface. This much we can deduce from only a casual examination of this one view. From the perspective we know immediately what the part looks like, in fact we see it here just about as it would appear were it placed on a table with one lip overhanging the edge, assuming of course, that it is of comparatively small size.

Fig. 10 shows the usual mechanical drawing of this same part. As you see, it is —and here it comes again—projected into the three views we've already learned

Just here it is well to note that there is an increasing tendency in the designing and drafting departments of many large manufacturers to use perspective views of parts and machines along with the projected mechanical drawings. And you can easily see how the combination would contribute to accuracy in reading the blueprints. The one helps to clarify the other and it is not necessary for the machinist to spend time and mental effort in visualizing a detailed assembly before he begins work. Combining the perspective and projected

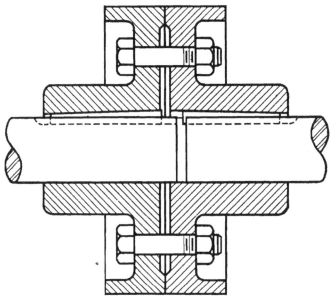

**Fig. 13A**

about. Notice how these drawings clear up the questions we've had about surface details when examining only the single perspective view. And if you go back and again look over the projected views of the box in Fig. 5 you can readily see that even though the surface features of the object become increasingly more intricate in detail, the projected views still show them clearly. Not only that, but if we add a title, telling what the part is, dimensions giving sizes and locations, machining data and kind of material and any other special notes necessary, we have a drawing containing all the information the machinist needs to make the part complete.

views reduces to the minimum the chance of error in interpreting the blueprints

**Cutting Planes:**

Cutting planes are intangible things They do not actually exist as something you can put your hand on. In Fig. 11, drawings A, B, and C, are imaginary "pictures" of cutting planes represented as cutting a square shape, a cone, and a cylinder respectively. A plane surface can be defined as any flat, uncurved surface but this definition is still rather loose and inconclusive. One would think of a table top as fulfilling the definition but seldom is a table top precisely flat. The point is that for

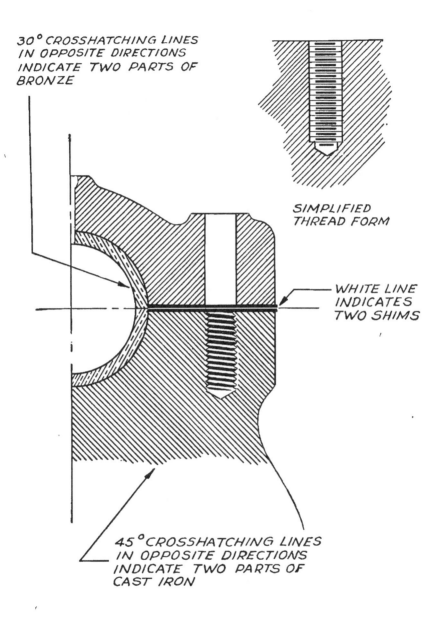

30° CROSSHATCHING LINES IN OPPOSITE DIRECTIONS INDICATE TWO PARTS OF BRONZE

SIMPLIFIED THREAD FORM

WHITE LINE INDICATES TWO SHIMS

45° CROSSHATCHING LINES IN OPPOSITE DIRECTIONS INDICATE TWO PARTS OF CAST IRON

SECTION THROUGH ASSEMBLED PARTS, FIG. 14

the moment we must think of the surface, any imaginary surface, as being absolutely flat. With this in mind and considering picture A, one simply thinks of the part as being cut in two at the point indicated by the imaginary plane surface in the picture A, and by the dot-dash line in the detail drawing at the right. Refer again to the line alphabet, Fig. 2, for the identity of the cutting-plane line as used in the latter detail. Another way to visualize it, perhaps more helpful to some students, is to think of the object A, Fig. 11, as being surrounded by horizontal and vertical continuous plane. The cutting-plane line may be continued at an angle or offset in several ways when this is necessary or advantageous in making a sectional view clearer. As an example, see Section A-A and B-B, Fig. 11A. Here, the cutting plane line locating section A-A is continued at an obtuse angle and is finally offset. In section B-B the line changes its direction three times.

**Material Sections:**

Supplementing the Symbols for Section Lining, Fig. 3, the material sections shown

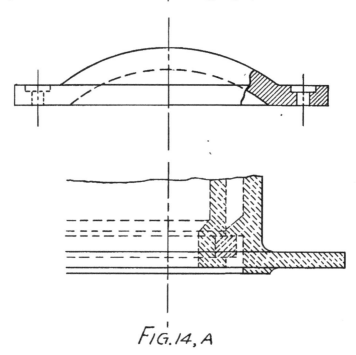

$Fig. 14, A$

planes coincident with the sides, top, and bottom surfaces, and the ends. Then think of another imaginary plane cutting these at any point along the length of the piece. Likewise, the imaginary plane can be made to cut the cone B, at any point. Obviously the same would be true of the cylindrical part, C.

Now, we've been thinking of cutting planes in general as imaginary flat surfaces at right angles to those of the object itself, the cutting plane lines running in one direction. However, it is not necessary that the cutting plane represent a single, in Fig. 12 are quite commonly used on certain types of drawings when these and all similar shapes are to be represented as either sectioned or broken. The eight symbols or conventions shown at the left in Fig. 12 are more especially used when breaks are to be shown in these particular material shapes. As can be readily seen, it would be impractical to crosshatch such sectional views as those of steel angles, I-beams, steel channels, and thin-walled tubing. Because of this, the sectional views of these shapes are generally shown as solid lines as indicated in the right-hand iews, Fig. 12. And, as it is convenient, the ame method is generally used in showing reaks in materials of these shapes as indicated in the left-hand views. The latter re really combination break and sectional iews as they indicate a b: eak and also 1ow a sectional view which determines 1e shape of the part without the necessity f making a separate drawing.

## ectional Views:

Without going into sections and sectional iews in great detail, they necessarily vary /ith each and every project, we can study ertain of those which are typical. Take he first one, A, in the top view, Fig. 13. 'his is an example of what 'is commonly eferred to as a "revolved" section, that is, he sectional view is drawn within the outne of the part with the cutting plane roated 45 degrees to present an end view f the part at that particular point. Here gain is an example of how the sectional iew clarifies the drawing and detailing of 1any machine parts. In fact, in this particular case, use of the revolved sections 1akes the single drawing sufficient to ompletely detail the shape and size of the ever with the single exception of the width f the eye bearing. Fig. 13, B, shows the ommon sectional views of a type of spring racket and at the same time brings up nother point of importance. Here the ection will pass directly through the web t its longitudinal center.

Following through with the conventions t would be necessary to crosshatch the veb as well as other adjacent parts. Of ourse, this would mean added time and abor in making the drawing and in addiion, might cause confusion in interpreting he relation of parts. So when he runs into his sort of thing the draftsman violates the onventions by omitting the crosshatching n such elements as ribs, webs, and simlar parts when the cutting plane passes hrough them in the same direction as they re located. If the section cuts the web or ther similar part at right angles then the arts would be crosshatched in the conventional manner as in the lower-right deail, Fig. 13, B. Essentially the same omision is made in the sectional view, Fig. 13, D. Also, drilled flanges in elevation or section hould show the holes at their true distance rom the center rather than the true pro-

jection. Fig. 13, D, is an example. Objects which are symmetrical in shape are often shown in what are known as "half sections." Fig. 13, C, is an example of this. Here one half the object, up to the center line, is shown in section, while the other half on the opposite side of the center line is shown in full. Sometimes the full half is omitted. This method halves the somewhat tedious work of section lining. Bolts and nuts, shafts, rods, keys, pins, and other similar parts whose axes lie directly in the cutting plane are not sectioned but are shown full, the sectional view in Fig. 13A being an example.

## Sections of More Than One Material:

Where sectional views include adjacent parts of the same material or of different materials it is regular practice not only to show the correct section lining symbol but to vary the direction of the lines so that the parts will "stand out," that is, they will easily be discernible to the reader when studying the drawing. Drawings in Fig. 13A and Fig. 14 are examples. In Fig. 13A it is obvious, even though the bolts and shafts were removed, that the flanged shapes are two separate parts. This is indicated by the section lining. In Fig. 14 we see much the same thing. The drawing could be that of a lathe headstock bearing, for example. Note that the shims between the main body and the cap and the two halves of the bronze bushing would easily be distinguishable even without the descriptive notes. Two variations in the method of showing screw threads are shown, one an older and more conventional method, the other a simplified form. As we shall see later, there is a further simplification being recommended in order to shorten the time necessary to draw representations of screw threads in detail, and also to make drawings more clear in certain cases. Fig. 14A, the upper view, shows what is generally called a "broken out" section. Note that this is distinguished from a "detail" section, Fig. 11A, because it is a section shown within the outlines of the object and not as a separate drawing. Sometimes, to avoid the necessity of making an extra view the draftsman uses what is generally called a "phantom" section. These are outside views with interior construction shown in section by means of

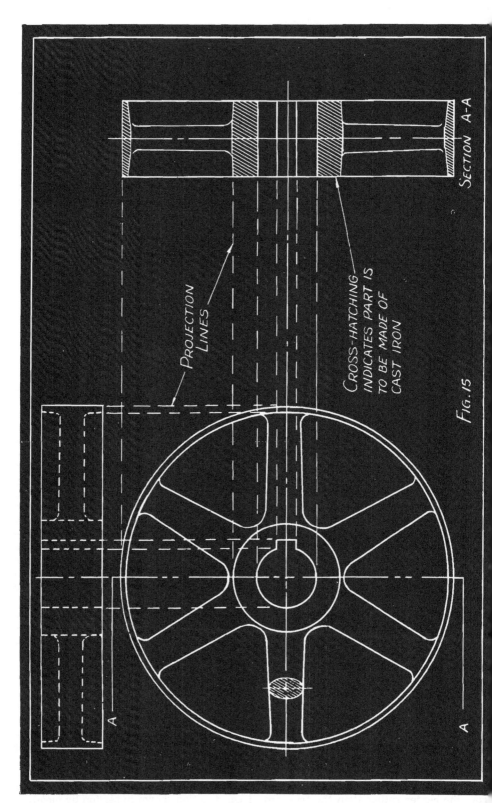

PROJECTION LINES

CROSS-HATCHING INDICATES PART IS TO BE MADE OF CAST IRON

SECTION A-A

FIG.15

34

otted crosshatching. The lower view, Fig. 4A is an example.

When the true or full projection of a part or parts requiring the section lining of ribs, webs, or arms might prove to be misleading, particularly in the circular object, the draftsman generally locates the cutting-plane line as in Fig. 15. Here, the arms of the pulley in the sectional view A-A are shown in full outline as the cutting-plane cuts only the rim and hub and the sectional view is completed with a revolved section of one arm. The label and note in Fig. 15 are included purposely in an effort to aid clarity and also to call attention to another of the points of current practice. The draftsman seldom relies exclusively on the character of the crosshatching alone to designate materials unless in special cases the graphic indication is so obvious as to require no reference letter or word. Usually, as has been remarked before, an opening is left in the section lining for the insertion of either a reference letter or word, the latter the name of the material, of course. Hence, you will not likely see notes such as that in Fig. 15 on blueprints. Nor will you see lines labeled "Projection lines"; neither is it often that you actually see the lines on present-day blueprints unless the latter are very complicated in detail. Thus, the note, lines, and label must be considered as merely explanatory and not a part of regular practice.

Just here is a good place to call attention to other applications of the same long-dash line which ordinarily is used to indicate an alternate position. When adjacent details are added to a drawing to indicate the position or use of the part represented the same symbol of long-dash lines is used as when showing the alternate position of parts. Refer again to Fig. 1. Also, this same line is used to show the position of bosses and lugs cast on parts for the purpose of holding them in a lathe chuck or other holding device while machining. Such lugs and bosses, or any similar projections are to be removed after the machine work is completed.

## Dimensions:

It's a cardinal rule in drafting room practice that all drawings of machine parts must be so completely dimensioned that the parts shown can be made without scaling the drawing or making any computations in order to obtain the measurements. Dimensions on the drawings must be those which are to be worked to in actual shop or constructional operations. Scaling is a practice which has never been generally recommended because of the ever-present chance of error in computing important dimensions. Because of the chance of misleading the blueprint reader, dimensions are not duplicated unless in exceptional cases they help to clarify the drawing. They must be arranged so that there will be no confusion as to their meaning or the part to which they refer. They must be grouped so that they are easily read at a glance. By this is meant that not only must the figures be clear and of uniform size but their respective dimension and extension lines must be so arranged as to leave no question concerning the part to which they refer.

Parts which can be measured with a standard rule or scale and which can be produced with sufficient accuracy to dimension in inches or the common fractions thereof are generally dimensioned in units and common fractions. Standard practice recommends that dimensions up to and including 72 inches should be expressed only in inches or fractions thereof, while generally, dimensions greater than 72 inches should be expressed in feet and inches, thus, $3'-3''$, $8'-0\frac{1}{2}''$, $8'-0''$. The dimensions stated in this way should be hyphenated as indicated above. On parts requiring a very fine finish or where fits require to be expressed in denominations which make common fractions inconvenient, then the dimensions are expressed in decimal fractions to at least three and often four places. Also, wire, sheet metal, structural sections, tubing walls, etc., are generally dimensioned in decimals. The commercial designation is also generally given in connection with measurements of such items. In structural drawing, dimensions of 12 inches and over are generally given in feet and inches. While in automotive, sheet metal, locomotive, and some others, all dimensions are usually exclusively specified in inches. When giving dimensions in inches and feet or where there are both inches and feet and inches denominations on the same drawing or se-

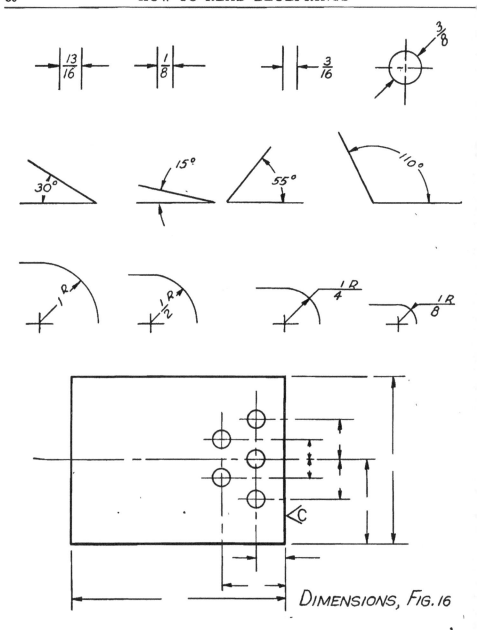

DIMENSIONS, FIG. 16

ries of drawings, sets, and the like, then the symbol (') is used to indicate feet while the symbol (") represents inches. On the other hand, when all dimensions are given in inches the symbol for inches is generally omitted when expressing the dimensions.

**Dimension Lines and Figures:**

Adding to what already has been said regarding dimension and extension lines we may mention in this connection several more common practices followed generally by draftsmen when making ordinary drawings. A dimension line does not pass through a dimension figure. The dimension line is broken for insertion of the dimension figure and when fractional dimensions are given, the numerator is placed above the dimension line and the denominator corresponding distance below it with the division line in line with the dimension line. Dimension lines and their corresponding figures are generally placed so that they may be read from the bottom or right-hand edges of the drawing. Extension lines indicate distances measured when the dimensions are placed outside the figure, that is, they are not generally placed within the outlines of the object. Leaders, lines leading from notes to designated points on the drawing with which the notes are directly concerned, are light solid lines terminated by arrowheads. As a rule they are not curved or made free hand but they are often made at an angle when this arrangement is more convenient. On structural drawings the dimension lines are generally made solid and the dimension figures are placed above the lines. Dimensions should be given from a base line, center line, or finished surface. Overall dimensions are placed outside all intermediate dimensions wherever possible, as in Fig. 16, the lower view. Frequently the draftsman finds it necessary to place dimensions in a limited space. When he runs into this problem he usually reverses the dimension lines by simply reversing the arrowheads in relation to the extension lines and places the dimension figure either between the extension lines or outside them as you see in the views in the upper row, Fig. 16.

One will usually find angles dimensioned as shown in Fig. 16 the second row from the top. Angles enclosing small areas are usually dimensioned by striking an arc with arrows touching the two legs and the dimension figure is placed either within the angle or outside so that it can be read from the horizontal position. An exception is shown when the angle includes a large area. Then the dimension is sometimes placed along the arc. Dimension lines, extension lines and dimension figures are not placed in crosshatched or shaded areas where possible to avoid it.

Dimensions indicating diameters are usually followed by the abbreviation "D" when the drawing does not show conclusively that that particular part or section is a circle or where the dimension is taken across a part whose outline is only a portion of a full circle. An example of this would be a length of round stock with two flats milled on opposite sides, or 180 de-

grees apart. A radius is generally dimensioned as shown in the third row of details, Fig. 16. The dimension is always followed by the abbreviation "R" and the center from which the measurement is taken is usually indicated by a cross or circle. The dimension line has only one arrowhead and this can be placed either inside or outside the arc as the space allows.

Now, note in passing, the "V" symbol in the lower detail, Fig. 16. This is a finish mark which has come into later use to largely, but not altogether, replace the earlier "f" symbol. Notice also that the V symbol carries a code letter which on the actual blueprint would refer to a note giving the degree or quality of finish required. As we shall see later on, this symbol will turn up again.

Fig. 17 shows two drawings, the forms of which make it necessary that dimensions group closely together. Notice carefully how the draftsman has handled the placing of the dimension and extension lines. And note, too, how the perpendicular center lines have been used as extension lines on both drawings. Dimension and extension lines giving the measurements of each surface feature are grouped in one direction from it so that when a machine set-up is made it is easy for the machinist to determine all the dimensions to be worked to on that particular surface. See the two upper views. In drawings of this particular type where a top and side view suffice, one should generally look for the overall lengthwise dimensions below the side view. It should be noted especially how the dimension line arrows are reversed with relation to the extension lines in the side view. In the top view, the extension lines are labeled at the inset. This has been done to call attention to a point in connection with the placing of extension lines. The extension lines do not touch the outlines, that is, the outlines of an object are not extended to form an extension line. The latter is always a separate lighter-bodied line. An extension line can cut through the outlines but should not in any way be a continuation of them.

Now, much of the above is simply an outline of general practice the draftsman follows in making drawings according to standard recommendations and the student of blueprint reading will do well to study

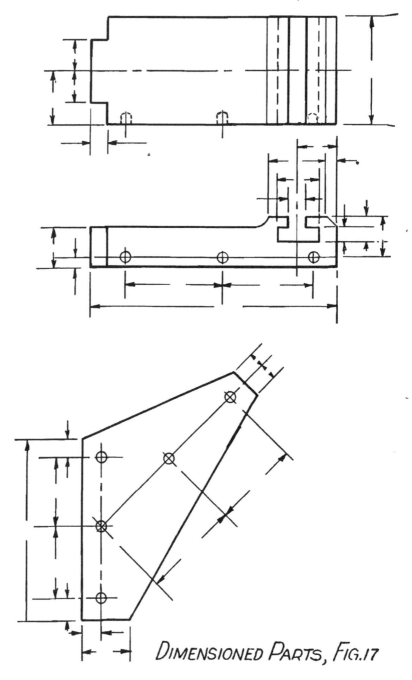

DIMENSIONED PARTS, FIG.17

them until he has the various points clearly in mind.

**Dimensioning Tapers:**

There are several methods of dimensioning tapers, and three are in common use.

The "taper per foot" is taken to mean the difference in diameter or width in one foot of length. Hence, one method gives one diameter, or width, and the length, and then a note is added on the drawing designating the taper by a number taken from tandard tables. The second method, where the slope is specified, gives the length and one diameter or diameters at both ends and omits the length. See Fig. 17A, for an example. In either internal or external precision work, the specifications usually give the slope and the diameter at a given distance from a surface.

## Dimensioning Curves and Angles:

There are two common methods of dimensioning curves. One is by means of a system of radii, the upper drawing in Fig. 18 being an example. Where the radial variation is not too great throughout the length this method is practical, that is, where not more than four to six radii are necessary to establish the path of the curved line this method is quite generally employed. Notice particularly how the

extension lines. At points where the radius shortens, the spacing between dimension lines is correspondingly lessened so that the curved line drawn through the fixed points will be regular.

Angular dimensions, such as those establishing either equally or unequally spaced points on the circumference of a circle or any part thereof or at any point within the circumference, are generally laid off from either a horizontal or vertical base line. Points are then located as required. Where equally-spaced holes are to be drilled it is common practice to locate only one and then add a note stating, for example, "Four holes equally spaced" or "Six holes equally spaced," and so on, as the case may be. The holes are then laid out in the shop with indexing plates or by other methods.

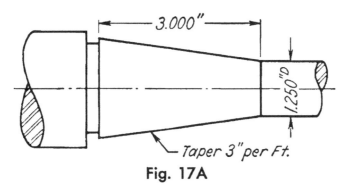

**Fig. 17A**

centers of the radii are dimensioned from a base line. Another method is that making use of a system of offsets. See the lower drawing in Fig. 18 which shows essentially the same curved shape as in the upper view. By this method practically any irregular curve can be accurately plotted and if a table of values is established for the offsets it is an easy matter to lay off the same curve on paper for the purpose of cutting a template, or directly on the surface of the work. Much the same system is used when developing the sheer lines in small-boat construction. As you see, distances are measured horizontally along a base line and on these points dimension lines are drawn perpendicular to the base line. The dimension line arrowheads touch the curved line at the respective points and the dimension lines are extended beyond the curved line to form

## Working Drawings:

Before we look at the simple working drawing it may be of help to recapitulate briefly and in part what we have already gone into. Thus far we have studied only the symbols and the more elemental practices and circumstances concerning the making of drawings, and how the blueprint reader is to interpret these representations. And in the last few paragraphs we have begun to investigate one of the principal reasons for making mechanical drawings, that is, that the drawing provides a means of accurately showing the size (dimensions) of an object, and listing and arranging this information in such a way that anyone with a knowledge of the meanings of lines, symbols, and characters used in making mechanical drawings could visualize the part or object represented and build it, providing, of course, the necessary

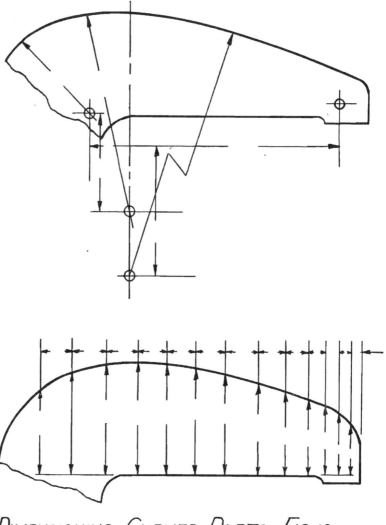

DIMENSIONING CURVED PARTS, FIG. 18

equipment was at hand, to measured sizes.

No working drawing is complete without dimensions of every part shown on it; in fact, without dimensions, it is not a working drawing at all. Nothing could be made from it to symmetrical size, nor could any part be made to fit any other part except by the doubtful process of "cut and try." Hence, in our American way of mass production of machines and parts of machines—some consisting of no more than half a dozen parts, others comprising hundreds and even thousands of precision parts machined within limits of measure-

ment so small that their accuracy can be checked only with special precision instruments and gages—accurate working drawings are of critical importance. They are, in a sense, the starting point, the master pattern from which operations are duplicated and interchangeable parts are multiplied times without number. They give form to the ideas of the machine designer and guide and direct the eye and hand and skill of the machinist to a definite end.

You will remember that we have already studied the relationship of the three views of an object. The top view, what you

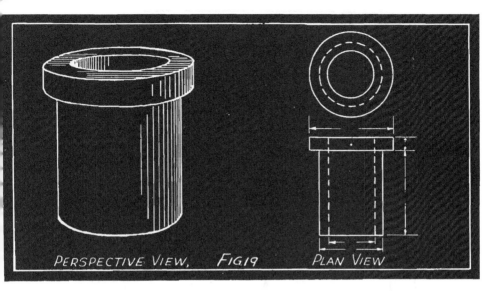

PERSPECTIVE VIEW,    FIG.19    PLAN VIEW

see when you look down on an object from a point directly above it, the side or front view, what you see when you look directly at the side of an object, and the end view, which is what you see when you look directly at the end. And you will recall also that some subjects require only two views while others may require four or more views in order to show the parts clearly and dimension them fully. When dimensions, explanatory notes, material specifications and any other necessary special information have been added to these arrangements of views we have a working drawing from which a machine or machine part can be made to specified size in the shop.

Fig. 19 shows such a drawing. It's an elementary one, but add a title, dimensions and a specification of material and, for ordinary purposes, it's complete. A perspective view is shown which, as has been remarked, is an increasing practice in many designing and drafting rooms. If you had a lathe at hand and a piece of material, we can assume for example that the part is a one-piece bushing of a flanged type, you could proceed to turn and bore the bushing from the rough to the specified dimensions.

Now, going a step farther and looking at Fig. 20 compare all three drawings in Fig. 19 and 20. In one of these the dimensions are incomplete, that is, the part is not fully dimensioned. Can you determine which one? It is, of course, the upper drawing in Fig. 20. Here you will see that only certain of the diameters are given. There are no overall or intermediate dimensions on the length of the part or of the steps. Hence, it is not a working drawing and is introduced just here for purposes of comparison, and also to call attention to a current practice of placing and writing dimensions. Note that there is no inch symbol (") from which one would deduce that all dimensions are given in inches. Also the letter "D" appears after each dimension which indicates that all dimensions given are diameters. In addition it will be noted that the dimensions are not placed in line but are staggered so that they may be more easily read. Furthermore, the part is shown in section which would indicate that it is perhaps more fully dimensioned elsewhere on a blueprint detailing several parts.

The lower drawing in Fig. 20 is complete in that it specifies all dimensions necessary to make the part. One new item turns up here which we have not seen heretofore. Size of the center hole is indicated by specifying the drill size in a note in place of dimensioning the hole in the usual way. See also Fig. 17A. Because of its convenience this practice is quite common. Also, note that again no inch symbol is shown and the "D" symbol is used on only one diameter. The larger diameter on this drawing is obvious but the smaller is not clearly seen in the edge view because two

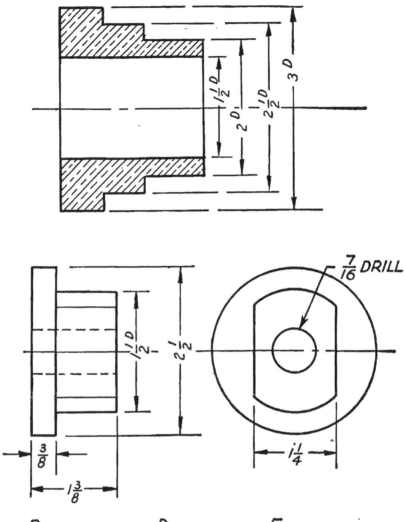

## DIMENSIONED DIAMETERS, FIG.20

flats are machined on opposite sides of the circular projection. Hence, the "D" symbol is used to indicate clearly that the dimension refers to a diameter.

Just here, in connection with these drawings detailing only a single part, it may be well to say that it is a quite common practice at present to detail only one or two parts on a single sheet of drawing paper. Thus the working drawings of a machine unit might cover many separate sheets and blueprints made from these drawings would be key-numbered as a set pertaining to that one machine. In this

way small sheets of a standard size can be used, crowding of detail is avoided and as a result the prints are easier to read. In many manufacturing plants one department will be charged with turning out one and sometimes several parts; another department, plant, or battery of machines will have the making of still another part and so on. This is more particularly true where assembly line methods are used in turning out the finished product. Of course not all plants, both large and small, operate in this way, for each has more or less worked out what for them appears to be the most effi-

cient procedure in solving individual production problems. Hence, in ordinary
work is it not so often that the blueprint
reader is called upon to visualize and carry
in mind the complete assembly of a complicated machine. Rather he is more likely
to be concerned directly with one or perhaps several of the parts. This should not
be taken too literally, however, for in
many cases it is necessary for the machinist to familiarize himself with every part
of the machine or assembly which is detailed in the blueprints in order that he
may work intelligently and efficiently on
parts with which he is directly concerned.

**Limit Dimensions:**

A limit dimension simply means that the
allowable error or "tolerance" as it is generally referred to, is definitely limited. It
means that the part can measure slightly
over the specified dimension or slightly
under to be acceptable or, in other words,
to pass inspection. Or it may mean that
the part cannot be over but can be slightly
under or vice versa, however the specification (dimension) may state. For example, suppose that a shaft is to be machined
to a diameter of 6.525D and the dimension
states that it cannot be over this diameter
but may be two-thousandths of an inch
under, thus the dimension, on parts where
few gages are used, ordinarily would be
written $6.525D \, {}^{+.000}_{-.002}$. That's only one way
of arranging the dimension, however. Fig.
21 shows other acceptable ways of expressing limit dimensions or tolerances.
On smaller parts where limit gages are to
be used the two values are usually placed
one above the other. For external dimensions of parts the maximum limit is placed
above the line while for internal dimensions the minimum limit is written above
the line. Compare the maximum tolerance
in the lower detail, Fig. 21, and the internal
dimension in Fig. 22. In the first, the maximum limit, referring to the external diameter, is placed above the line while in the
latter, referring to the internal diameter,
the minimum tolerance is written above
the line. Fig. 22A is another example of
how tolerance dimensions are handled
when there are a number of operations to
be performed on a single part. Notice that
the larger diameter is cored to a dimension

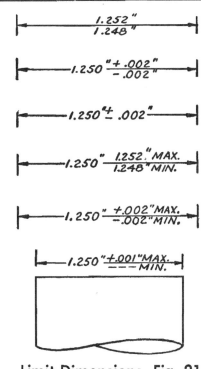

## Limit Dimensions, Fig. 21

of 2 inches; the second diameter is rough
bored to 1¾ inches, but the third diameter
has a rough bore, a finish bore, and a final-
grind dimension, the latter a finish within
fairly close limits, .002 or two thousandths
of an inch, in fact.

Now, in Fig. 22 the "V" finish mark*,
already mentioned, turns up again. A finish mark is simply a symbol used by the
draftsman to direct the attention of the
workman, also the blueprint reader in
whatever capacity he may be, to the degree
or quality of finish on certain surfaces of
the work. In the older practice employing
the "f" symbol or mark, where certain
parts in their entirety or several surfaces
or shapes of a single part separated from
the balance were to be finished from the
rough, a term referring to the surface condition of an unfinished casting or forging,
a note would be added to the drawing thus,
**"f" all over.** In other cases, where only one
surface or a bottom and top or side were
to be finished, the "f" symbol would be

* A standard set of symbols for use with the "V" marks is
now being developed by the Sectional Committee on Stand-
ardization of Classification and Designation of Surface
Qualities (B46) organized under the procedure of the ASA
with the A S M E and the S A E. as joint sponsor bodies.

placed directly on the outline of the surface to be finished and a note would specify the degree or quality of finish required. Some drafting rooms still follow this practice. When using the newer "V" mark it is a common practice to draw a 60-degree "V" with the bottom of the "V" touching the outline as shown. Then a key letter or figure is placed within the "V." This will usually refer to notes placed at the bottom or side of the drawings, which specify the degree and quality of the finish.

**Notes:**

Drawings in Fig. 22A and Fig. 23 show several ways in which notes are commonly used in place of figure dimensions alone. This not only simplifies the drawing but makes it easier to read with consequently less chance of error. Notes are used more particularly where it is necessary to specify the performance and dimensions of a number of machine operations on the same

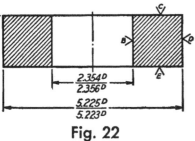

**Fig. 22**

part. The four sectional drawings in Fig. 23 deal with the drilling and finishing of counterbored and countersunk holes. Note carefully the variations. Diameters and depths are given for the countersunk holes. In one case, referring to countersunk holes, the drill size and the degree of the angle of the countersink is given as a note, while in another, the drill is specified in a note while the angle of the countersink is given in a figure dimension. Another gives the drill size, the size of the counterbore, the depth of the counterbore and the number of holes to be finished all in a single note. All sizes are in common fractions and no figure dimensions or dimension lines are used at all. The lower drawing in Fig. 23 shows another variation. Here only one dimension line is given but the rough turn, finish turn and finish-

grind diameters are specified. And only the maximum and minimum tolerances are given. Therefore, there is no calculated fixed size indicated. Ordinarily then, it would mean that the first dimension is to be held within limits of 3.250 and 3.240 in. and that in the final dimension either 3.171, 3.170 or 3.169 in. would be acceptable. However it should perhaps be noted that it is nearly always implied that the exact dimension is the size the workman should strive for, unless, of course, the limitations of time, place, nature of work or other factors make it necessary that he merely hold the work somewhere within the limits specified.

In connection with notes, limit dimensions and figure dimensions it should be remarked that on drawings where dimensions must be changed after completion of the drawing, the changed figures are usually either underscored or located with a letter or number placed adjacent to the altered dimension. The letter, figure, or other symbol usually refers to a tabulation elsewhere on the drawing giving reasons for the change or whatever other information is necessary.

As we shall see later on, it is the practice of many manufacturers, who either maintain their own drafting rooms, or have the work done by draftsmen who work in close touch with their designing and production departments, to use a standard size sheet of drawing or tracing paper, on each sheet of which is printed a "running" title box and quite often a note designating the tolerances, fits or other limits which are adopted as standard for the class and type of work they are doing or intend to do. Hence, the notes are generally worded to mean that dimensions pertaining to fits, tolerances or other limits are to be held within the figure given in the note unless otherwise stated on the drawing. Usually such single sheets detail only one or two parts and often each sheet is key-numbered or otherwise identified in connection with an assembly drawing of the completed machine.

Now, to sum up, it is essential that the student of blueprint reading make an especially careful study of dimensions and particularly the various ways of expressing them. The drawing alone is merely one type of "picture" of the object; the dimensions are a "shorthand" way of stating the action, the work to be done on the part pictured by the drawing. They state the "when," "where" and "how much." One can think of these as terms expressing action. By reading the dimensions alone an experienced machinist will get a clear general idea of the type of machining he must do, the machine setups he must use and the bench layout work he must do in connection with making the part or parts to the specifications called for. Dimensions, like the lines, are a part of the "shorthand" vocabulary of the blueprint.

are permitted to take up considerable space even on working drawings. Explanatory notes and locating data are generally a part of assembly, machinery and location drawings. But always the draftsman tries to avoid "cluttering" a drawing with any lettering or grouping of lettering other than the bare essentials. Charts showing specimens of the two types of lettering commonly used appear in Figs. 24 and 25. Legibility is the essential requirement in lettering on any drawing. What is generally known as the single stroke gothic letter in either the vertical or inclined style

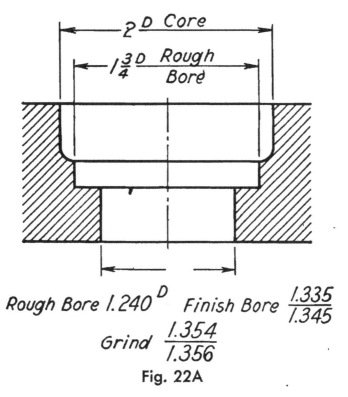

Fig. 22A

## Lettering:

The type of lettering on the drawings is of only indirect concern to the blueprint reader. That is the draftsman's job. But it is perhaps well for the student to know something of the general practices of the draftsman in lettering drawings.

It is a quite general aim to avoid profuse lettering on any working drawing except where lengthy explanatory notes are essential to clarity. Frequently material lists

has the preference as it is easy to read through a wide range of size and is rapidly executed either free hand or with the aid of a lettering guide. The slanting style is perhaps more generally used by the draftsman because it is somewhat easier to do free hand. As you can see from Figs. 24 and 25, each group of lettering states its own purpose and place as commonly used on the blueprint. Ordinarily lettering is not graded according to the size of the

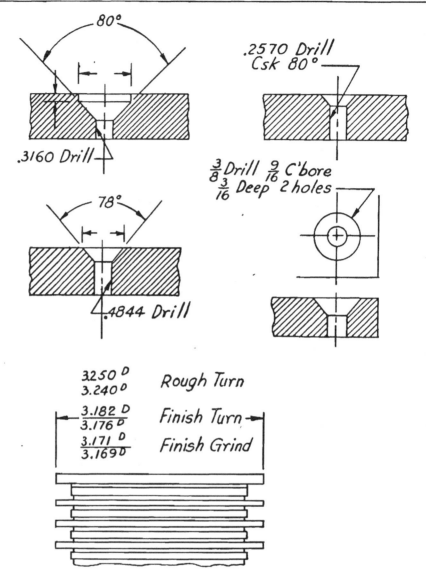

DIMENSIONS SPECIFIED BY NOTES, FIG. 23

drawing but is kept to a standard height which is easy to execute and which is readily legible. Of course, size and weight of lettering must always be sufficient to produce legible prints from tracings done in either ink or pencil. One exception is where reproductions of prints are to be made by a photographic process. Then it is frequently necessary to make certain variations in the size of the lettering in order to achieve the desired result in a print either reduced or enlarged from an original. Lettering is not ordinarily underlined except in instances when unusual emphasis is desirable. Use of a lettering guide is quite common practice when neatness is a special requirement.

**Screw Threads:**

One elementary definition of a screw thread is that usually it is simply an advancing spiral cut into the surface of a

*ABCDEFGHIJKLMNOP*
*QRSTUVWXYZ&*
*1234567890* $\frac{1}{2}$ $\frac{3}{4}$ $\frac{5}{8}$ $\frac{7}{16}$
*TO BE USED FOR MAIN TITLES*
*& DRAWING NUMBERS*

TYPE 2 *ABCDEFGHIJKLMNOPQR*
*STUVWXYZ&*
*1234567890* $\frac{13}{64}$ $\frac{5}{8}$ $\frac{1}{2}$
*TO BE USED FOR SUB-TITLES*

TYPE 3 *ABCDEFGHIJKLMNOPQRSTUVWXYZ&*
*1234567890* $\frac{1}{2}$ $\frac{3}{4}$ $\frac{5}{8}$ $\frac{7}{16}$
*FOR HEADINGS AND PROMINENT NOTES*

TYPE 4 *ABCDEFGHIJKLMNOPQRSTUVWXYZ&*
*1234567890* $\frac{1}{2}$ $\frac{3}{4}$ $\frac{5}{8}$ $\frac{7}{16}$ $\frac{1}{32}$ $\frac{1}{8}$
*FOR BILLS OF MATERIAL, DIMENSIONS & GENERAL NOTES*

TYPE 5
*OPTIONAL TYPE SAME AS TYPE 4 BUT USING TYPE 3 FOR FIRST*
*LETTER OF PRINCIPAL WORDS. MAY BE USED FOR SUB-TITLES &*
*NOTES ON THE BODY OF DRAWINGS.*

TYPE 6 *abcdefghijklmnopqrstuvwxyz*
*Type 6 may be used in place of*
*Type 4 with capitals of Type 3,*
*for Bills of Material and Notes*
*on Body of Drawing.*

**Fig. 24**

cylinder, having a regular sectional form throughout its length and a given amount of pitch or advance in a single full turn of the cylinder. In the last few years considerable change in the naming, designating and specifying of screw threads has taken place. While it is true that in essential the older forms of threads remain, modern practice directs much more attention to fit. Hence, greater importance is attached to pitch diameter, lead, and the angle of the thread. This concerns the intentional al-

# ABCDEFGHIJKLMNOP QRSTUVWXYZ&
# 1234567890 $\frac{1}{2}\frac{3}{4}\frac{5}{8}$
## TITLES & DRAWING NUMBERS

TYPE 2

## FOR SUB-TITLES OR MAIN TITLES ON SMALL DRAWINGS

TYPE 3   ABCDEFGHIJKLMNOPQRSTUVWXYZ&

1234567890 $\frac{1}{2}\frac{3}{4}\frac{5}{8}\frac{9}{32}$

### FOR HEADINGS AND PROMINENT NOTES

TYPE 4      ABCDEFGHIJKLMNOPQRSTUVWXYZ&

1234567890 $\frac{1}{2}\frac{3}{4}\frac{5}{8}\frac{23}{64}$

FOR BILLS OF MATERIAL, DIMENSIONS & GENERAL NOTES

TYPE 5

OPTIONAL TYPE SAME AS TYPE 4 BUT USING TYPE 3 FOR FIRST LETTER OF PRINCIPAL WORDS. MAY BE USED FOR SUB-TITLES AND NOTES ON THE BODY OF DRAWINGS.

4

**Fig. 25**

lowances, or perhaps more properly, the interferences between the engaging surfaces of threads in and on two separate parts. Heretofore, standards considered form, outside diameter, and pitch.

There is a close analogy between the characteristics and dimensional specifications of screw threads and gears. The outside and root diameters of screw threads are considered unimportant except that the thread must not bear either on the root or crest. Essentially the same thing is true of engaging gear teeth. Were this condition brought about either by design or error neither the threads nor the gears would be of any practical use. The pitch diameter of the thread is of the greatest importance to the fit, and the same is true of gears. The lead is likewise important as is the tooth spacing in gears.

Along with the new emphasis on accu-

racy there had to come a more precise method of measuring threads. The lead of a single screw thread is usually defined as the distance a thread will advance or move forward in one full turn of the screw. In a single-threaded screw pitch and lead are equal so the screw will advance only one thread, or perhaps more clearly, it will move from one thread to the next in one turn of the screw. But a double-threaded screw will advance two threads, or in other words, the lead equals twice the pitch. The word "pitch" should not be used in referring to the number of threads per inch. For example, it is not considered correct in recommended practice to refer to a screw having 12 threads per inch as a 12-pitch thread.

What is now known and designated as the American Standard Thread Form was formerly the U. S. Standard. Figs. 27 and

# American Standard Screw Thread Definitions

**Major Diameter:** The largest diameter of a screw thread. The term major diameter applies to both internal and external threads and replaces the term "outside diameter" as applied to the thread of a screw and also the term "full diameter" as applied to the thread of a nut.

**Minor Diameter:** The smallest diameter of a screw thread. The term minor diameter applies to both internal and external threads and replaces the terms "core diameter" and "root diameter" as applied to the thread of a screw and also the term "inside diameter" as applied to the thread of a nut.

**Pitch Diameter:** The diameter of an imaginary cylinder the surface of which would pass through the threads at such points as to make equal the width of the threads and the width of the spaces cut by the surface of the cylinder.

**Pitch:** The distance from a point on a screw thread to a corresponding point on the next thread measured parallel to the axis.

**Lead:** The distance a screw thread advances axially in one turn. On a single-thread screw, the lead and pitch are identical; on a double-thread screw, the lead is twice the pitch; on a triple-thread screw, the lead is three times the pitch, etc.

**Angle of Thread:** The angle included between the sides of the thread measured in an axial plane.

**Helix Angle:** The angle made by the helix of the thread at the pitch diameter with a plane perpendicular to the axis.

**Crest:** The top surface joining the two sides of a thread.

**Root:** The bottom surface joining the sides of two adjacent threads.

**Depth of Thread:** The distance between the crest and the root of thread measured normal to the axis.

**Depth of Engagement:** The depth of thread contact of two mating parts, measured radially.

**Basic:** The theoretical or nominal standard size from which all variations are made.

**Crest Clearance:** Defined on a screw form as the space between the crest of a thread and the root of its mating thread.

**Allowance:** An intentional difference in the dimensions of mating parts. It is the minimum clearance or the maximum interference which is intended between mating parts.

**Tolerance:** The amount of variation permitted in the size of a part.

**Neutral Zone:** A positive allowance. (See "Allowance.")

**Limits:** The extreme permissible dimensions of a part.

## Fig. 26

28 give basic measurements of the American Standard Coarse (NC) and the American Standard Fine (NF). The symbols "NC" and "NF" have been retained from former designations. There are also other symbols used in special specifications of screw thread series.

To get an idea of the meaning and applications of screw thread terms the student should make a careful study of Figs. 26 and 29. Of all these definitions and their practical applications and meanings perhaps the most difficult to get clearly in mind is the meaning of the pitch diameter. It is perhaps as difficult to state as it is to visualize, but we may venture a rather crude example which might possibly prove helpful in getting the general meaning in mind. If one visualizes a screw thread cut on the surface of a cylinder and another hollow cylindrical shape, such as a length of tubing, forced over the first so that it figuratively shears off the top half of the threads, that is, cuts them approximately half way between the minor and major diameters, one can perhaps grasp more clearly the meaning of the definition of the pitch diameter, as given in Fig. 26. This theoretical operation leaves only half the normal height of the threads remaining on

### Table 1. American Standard Screw Threads — Coarse-thread Series
The Coarse-Thread Series is recommended for general use.  See footnote

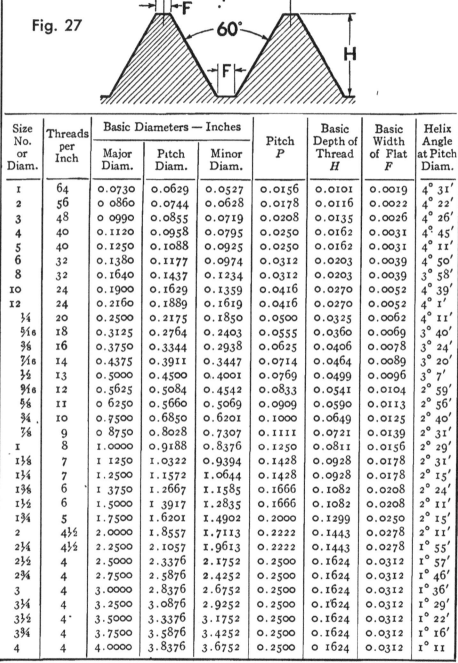

Fig. 27

| Size No. or Diam. | Threads per Inch | Basic Diameters — Inches | | | Pitch P | Basic Depth of Thread H | Basic Width of Flat F | Helix Angle at Pitch Diam. |
|---|---|---|---|---|---|---|---|---|
| | | Major Diam. | Pitch Diam. | Minor Diam. | | | | |
| 1 | 64 | 0.0730 | 0.0629 | 0.0527 | 0.0156 | 0.0101 | 0.0019 | 4° 31' |
| 2 | 56 | 0 0860 | 0.0744 | 0.0628 | 0.0178 | 0.0116 | 0.0022 | 4° 22' |
| 3 | 48 | 0 0990 | 0.0855 | 0.0719 | 0.0208 | 0.0135 | 0.0026 | 4° 26' |
| 4 | 40 | 0.1120 | 0.0958 | 0.0795 | 0.0250 | 0.0162 | 0.0031 | 4° 45' |
| 5 | 40 | 0.1250 | 0.1088 | 0.0925 | 0.0250 | 0.0162 | 0.0031 | 4° 11' |
| 6 | 32 | 0.1380 | 0.1177 | 0.0974 | 0.0312 | 0.0203 | 0.0039 | 4° 50' |
| 8 | 32 | 0.1640 | 0.1437 | 0.1234 | 0.0312 | 0.0203 | 0.0039 | 3° 58' |
| 10 | 24 | 0.1900 | 0.1629 | 0.1359 | 0.0416 | 0.0270 | 0.0052 | 4° 39' |
| 12 | 24 | 0.2160 | 0.1889 | 0.1619 | 0.0416 | 0.0270 | 0.0052 | 4° 1' |
| ¼ | 20 | 0.2500 | 0.2175 | 0.1850 | 0.0500 | 0.0325 | 0.0062 | 4° 11' |
| 5⁄16 | 18 | 0.3125 | 0.2764 | 0.2403 | 0.0555 | 0.0360 | 0.0069 | 3° 40' |
| 3⁄8 | 16 | 0.3750 | 0.3344 | 0.2938 | 0.0625 | 0.0406 | 0.0078 | 3° 24' |
| 7⁄16 | 14 | 0.4375 | 0.3911 | 0.3447 | 0.0714 | 0.0464 | 0.0089 | 3° 20' |
| ½ | 13 | 0.5000 | 0.4500 | 0.4001 | 0.0769 | 0.0499 | 0.0096 | 3° 7' |
| 9⁄16 | 12 | 0.5625 | 0.5084 | 0.4542 | 0.0833 | 0.0541 | 0.0104 | 2° 59' |
| 5⁄8 | 11 | 0 6250 | 0.5660 | 0.5069 | 0.0909 | 0.0590 | 0.0113 | 2° 56' |
| ¾ | 10 | 0.7500 | 0.6850 | 0.6201 | 0.1000 | 0.0649 | 0.0125 | 2° 40' |
| 7⁄8 | 9 | 0 8750 | 0.8028 | 0.7307 | 0.1111 | 0.0721 | 0.0139 | 2° 31' |
| 1 | 8 | 1.0000 | 0.9188 | 0.8376 | 0.1250 | 0.0811 | 0.0156 | 2° 29' |
| 1⅛ | 7 | 1 1250 | 1.0322 | 0.9394 | 0.1428 | 0.0928 | 0.0178 | 2° 31' |
| 1¼ | 7 | 1.2500 | 1.1572 | 1.0644 | 0.1428 | 0.0928 | 0.0178 | 2° 15' |
| 1⅜ | 6 | 1 3750 | 1.2667 | 1.1585 | 0.1666 | 0.1082 | 0.0208 | 2° 24' |
| 1½ | 6 | 1.5000 | 1 3917 | 1.2835 | 0.1666 | 0.1082 | 0.0208 | 2° 11' |
| 1¾ | 5 | 1.7500 | 1.6201 | 1.4902 | 0.2000 | 0.1299 | 0.0250 | 2° 15' |
| 2 | 4½ | 2.0000 | 1.8557 | 1.7113 | 0.2222 | 0.1443 | 0.0278 | 2° 11' |
| 2¼ | 4½ | 2.2500 | 2.1057 | 1.9613 | 0.2222 | 0.1443 | 0.0278 | 1° 55' |
| 2½ | 4 | 2.5000 | 2.3376 | 2.1752 | 0.2500 | 0.1624 | 0.0312 | 1° 57' |
| 2¾ | 4 | 2.7500 | 2.5876 | 2.4252 | 0.2500 | 0.1624 | 0.0312 | 1° 46' |
| 3 | 4 | 3.0000 | 2.8376 | 2.6752 | 0.2500 | 0.1624 | 0.0312 | 1° 36' |
| 3¼ | 4 | 3.2500 | 3.0876 | 2.9252 | 0.2500 | 0.1624 | 0.0312 | 1° 29' |
| 3½ | 4· | 3.5000 | 3.3376 | 3.1752 | 0.2500 | 0.1624 | 0.0312 | 1° 22' |
| 3¾ | 4 | 3.7500 | 3.5876 | 3.4252 | 0.2500 | 0.1624 | 0.0312 | 1° 16' |
| 4 | 4 | 4.0000 | 3.8376 | 3.6752 | 0.2500 | 0 1624 | 0.0312 | 1° 11 |

The form of thread profile for all American Standard threads is designated as the American National Form (see diagram above table), and it is the same as the profile previously known as the United States Standard.  This revised standard was approved by the American Standards Association, April, 1935.

## Table 2. American Standard Screw Threads — Fine-thread Series

The Fine-Thread Series is recommended for use where special conditions require a fine thread

| Size No. or Diam. | Threads per Inch | Basic Diameters — Inches | | | Pitch P | Basic Depth of Thread H | Basic Width of Flat F | Helix Angle at Pitch Diam. |
|---|---|---|---|---|---|---|---|---|
| | | Major Diam. | Pitch Diam. | Minor Diam. | | | | |
| 0 | 80 | 0.0600 | 0.0519 | 0.0438 | 0.0125 | 0.0081 | 0.0015 | 4° 23' |
| 1 | 72 | 0.0730 | 0.0640 | 0.0550 | 0.0139 | 0.0090 | 0.0017 | 3° 57' |
| 2 | 64 | 0.0860 | 0.0759 | 0.0657 | 0.0156 | 0.0101 | 0.0019 | 3° 45' |
| 3 | 56 | 0.0990 | 0.0874 | 0.0758 | 0.0178 | 0.0116 | 0.0022 | 3° 43' |
| 4 | 48 | 0.1120 | 0.0985 | 0.0849 | 0.0208 | 0.0135 | 0.0026 | 3° 51' |
| 5 | 44 | 0.1250 | 0.1102 | 0.0955 | 0.0227 | 0.0147 | 0.0028 | 3° 45' |
| 6 | 40 | 0.1380 | 0.1218 | 0.1055 | 0.0250 | 0.0162 | 0.0031 | 3° 44' |
| 8 | 36 | 0.1640 | 0.1460 | 0.1279 | 0.0278 | 0.0180 | 0.0035 | 3° 28' |
| 10 | 32 | 0.1900 | 0.1697 | 0.1494 | 0.0312 | 0.0203 | 0.0039 | 3° 21' |
| 12 | 28 | 0.2160 | 0.1928 | 0.1696 | 0.0357 | 0.0232 | 0.0044 | 3° 22' |
| ¼ | 28 | 0.2500 | 0.2268 | 0.2036 | 0.0357 | 0.0232 | 0.0044 | 2° 52' |
| ⁵⁄₁₆ | 24 | 0.3125 | 0.2854 | 0.2584 | 0.0416 | 0.0270 | 0.0052 | 2° 40' |
| ⅜ | 24 | 0.3750 | 0.3479 | 0.3209 | 0.0416 | 0.0270 | 0.0052 | 2° 11' |
| ⁷⁄₁₆ | 20 | 0.4375 | 0.4050 | 0.3725 | 0.0500 | 0.0325 | 0.0062 | 2° 15' |
| ½ | 20 | 0.5000 | 0.4675 | 0.4350 | 0.0500 | 0.0325 | 0.0062 | 1° 57' |
| ⁹⁄₁₆ | 18 | 0.5625 | 0.5264 | 0.4903 | 0.0555 | 0.0361 | 0.0069 | 1° 55' |
| ⅝ | 18 | 0.6250 | 0.5889 | 0.5528 | 0.0555 | 0.0361 | 0.0069 | 1° 43' |
| ¾ | 16 | 0.7500 | 0.7094 | 0.6688 | 0.0625 | 0.0406 | 0.0078 | 1° 36' |
| ⅞ | 14 | 0.8750 | 0.8286 | 0.7822 | 0.0714 | 0.0464 | 0.0089 | 1° 34' |
| 1 | 14 | 1.0000 | 0.9536 | 0.9072 | 0.0714 | 0.0464 | 0.0089 | 1° 22' |
| 1⅛ | 12 | 1.1250 | 1.0709 | 1.0167 | 0.0833 | 0.0541 | 0.0104 | 1° 25' |
| 1¼ | 12 | 1.2500 | 1.1959 | 1.1417 | 0.0833 | 0.0541 | 0.0104 | 1° 16' |
| 1⅜ | 12 | 1.3750 | 1.3209 | 1.2667 | 0.0833 | 0.0541 | 0.0104 | 1° 9' |
| 1½ | 12 | 1.5000 | 1.4459 | 1 3917 | 0.0833 | 0.0541 | 0.0104 | 1° 3' |

### Fig. 28

he cylinder, the width of the flats thus ormed being equal to the spaces between. With this illustration in mind the details n Fig. 29 may possibly have a clearer meaning. Note carefully the upper sectional view and the center view, the former s that of an internal thread while the later represents an external thread, that is, a screw thread cut on the surface of a cylinder, a bolt, for example. The top view represents the thread on an interior surface, such as the nut. You can see that the major diameters reverse position in the two views, that is, the major diameter is measured at the root of the thread instead of at the crest as in the center view. This point should be kept in mind to avoid confusion.

As has already been remarked, the most important dimension of the screw thread is the pitch diameter, sometimes referred to as the "effective" diameter. So it is very necessary that there be precise means of establishing this dimension. The two methods shown in Fig. 30 are in quite common use for ordinary purposes. There are also others. In critical precision work an optical method is widely used. However, the screw-thread micrometer, top view, Fig. 30, is considered sufficiently accurate for the ordinary run of thread measurement. This instrument is especially made for the purpose, the anvil being V-shaped to engage a single thread in the manner shown. The sloping outer sides bear against the slopes of the two adjacent threads. The

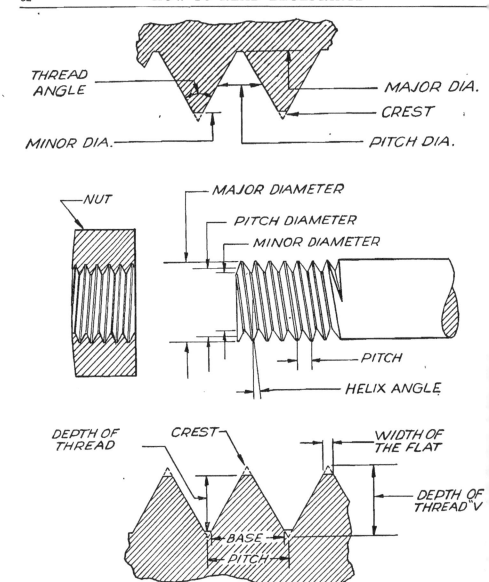

THREAD ANGLE

MAJOR DIA.

CREST

MINOR DIA.

PITCH DIA.

NUT

MAJOR DIAMETER

PITCH DIAMETER

MINOR DIAMETER

PITCH

HELIX ANGLE

DEPTH OF THREAD

CREST

WIDTH OF THE FLAT

DEPTH OF THREAD "V"

BASE

PITCH

SCREW THREAD TERMS, FIG. 29

cone-shaped point of the spindle enters the space between two threads as indicated. Now in order to determine the pitch diameter of the thread accurately it is necessary that the sloping sides of the micrometer anvil and spindle contact only the sides of the threads and clear at the root and crest. Hence clearances are allowed on both the anvil and spindle to prevent the spindle bearing on the bottom of the thread and the anvil from bearing on the top the thread. The pointed spindle is adapt to measuring all threads within the capacity of the "mike" but to cover a wide range of thread pitches, interchangeable anvils of varying sizes are required, course. Once the measurement is taken is compared with tables giving three depths of the American or other standard The second method makes use of a

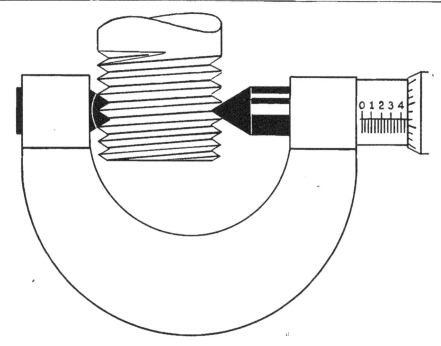

*THREAD MICROMETER*

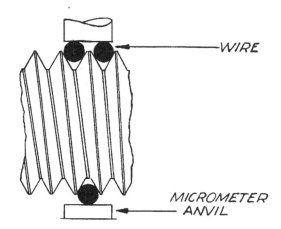

*WIRE*

*MICROMETER ANVIL*

*THREE WIRE METHOD*

*THREAD MEASUREMENT, FIG.30*

rdinary micrometer with right-angled nvil and spindle and three wires placed etween the threads in the position indiated in the lower view, Fig. 30. The method is more particularly used in checking ccuracy of threads on gages and other neasuring instruments. In extremely fine precision work a "floating" micrometer is often used to take these measurements. The screw is held between centers as in a lathe and the mike is mounted on a slide having motions both parallel and at right angles to the axis of the screw. In this case only two wires are used as the mike is

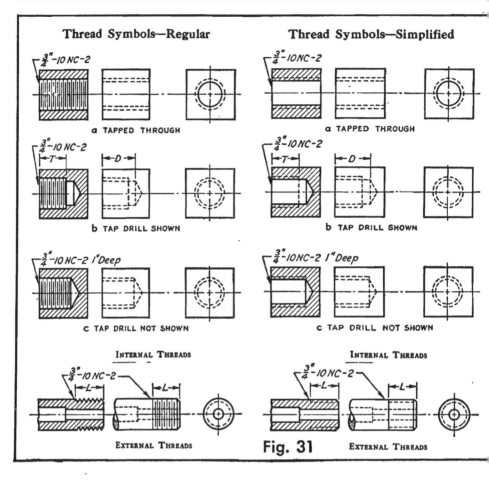

**Thread Symbols—Regular**

**Thread Symbols—Simplified**

a TAPPED THROUGH

b TAP DRILL SHOWN

c TAP DRILL NOT SHOWN

INTERNAL THREADS

EXTERNAL THREADS

**Fig. 31**

always held at right angles to the work by the slide on which it is mounted. The third wire is necessary to keep the mike at right angles to the axis of the screw when it is held freehand. By either method it is necessary that the micrometer reading for wires of a given size be known and that the wires used be of equal size.

**Screw Thread Symbols:**

There are two symbolic representations of screw threads generally approved for use at the present time, known as the "Regular" and the "Simplified" forms, Fig. 31. The latter form has been developed and approved for the purpose of simplifying representations of screw threads on both detail and assembly drawings. Use of this form greatly shortens the draftsman's time on drawings involving the representation of numbers of screw threads. Of course,

the regular form is still in quite common use. In this form threads are represented by alternating cross lines of two lengths, the longer line indicating the crests and the shorter heavier line the roots of the thread. These lines are drawn at right angles to the axis of the screw and do not represent the pitch. Exceptions are the sectional views of external and internal threads, the latter being invisible, of course. If desired, the lines can be of the same weight. If you study the regular and simplified symbols in Fig. 31 you can see how external screw threads and threads in tapped holes are shown by the two methods. Notice particularly a, b, and c. First the hole tapped clear through is shown in the regular and simplified forms. Then the tap drill is indicated, b, and you will notice that the depth of both the tap drill and the tap are indicated. A regular tap is to

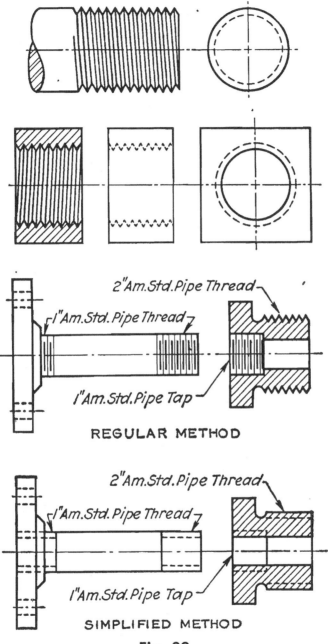

2"Am.Std.Pipe Thread

1"Am.Std.Pipe Thread

1"Am.Std.Pipe Tap

REGULAR METHOD

2"Am.Std.Pipe Thread

1"Am.Std.Pipe Thread

1"Am.Std.Pipe Tap

SIMPLIFIED METHOD

Fig. 32

be used in both these holes. Finally, the method shown in Fig. 31, c, is to be used when it is desired to indicate the use of a bottoming tap. Here the tap drill is not shown. By the simplified method both internal and external threads are indicated merely by drawing short-dash lines parallel to the axis of the screw, the lines indicating the depth and extent of the thread. Note that in each case the size and length of the thread is to be given either as a note or as a note and conventional dimension.

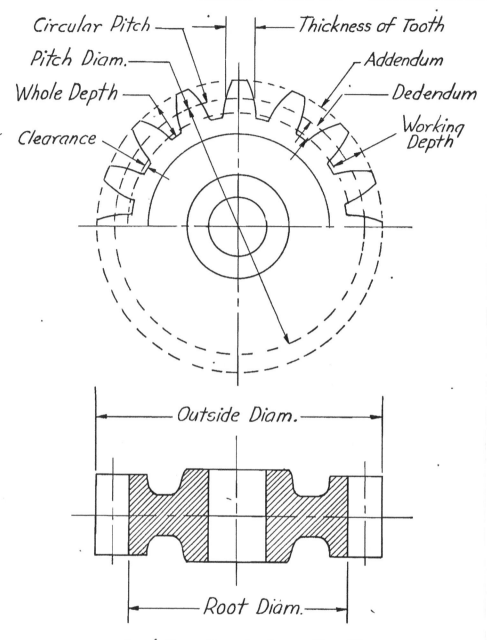

**Spur Gear Terminology, Fig. 33**

The simplified method is not used in sectional views of assembled parts. Unless otherwise stated on the drawing threads are always assumed to be right-hand. Left-hand threads are usually designated by the abbreviation "LH."

**Pipe Threads:**

Pipe threads are represented in essentially the same manner on drawings as are bolt threads. As you see from the two lower views in Fig. 32 they are represented

(Continued to page 58)

# Definitions of Gear Terms

**Addendum:** Height of tooth above pitch circle or the radial distance between the pitch circle and the top of the tooth.

**Arc of action:** Arc of a pitch circle through which a tooth travels from the first point of contact with the mating tooth to the point where contact ceases.

**Arc of approach:** Arc of the pitch circle through which a tooth travels from the first point of contact with the mating tooth to the pitch point.

**Arc of recession:** Arc of the pitch circle through which a tooth travels from its contact with the mating tooth at the pitch point to the point where its contact ceases.

**Backlash:** The play between mating teeth or the shortest distance between the non-driving surfaces of adjacent teeth.

**Base circle:** The circle from which an involute tooth curve is generated or developed.

**Chordal addendum:** The radial distance from a line representing the chordal thickness at the pitch circle to the top of the tooth.

**Chordal thickness:** Length of the chord subtended by the circular thickness arc (the dimension obtained when a gear-tooth caliper is used to measure the thickness at the pitch circle).

**Circular pitch:** Length of the arc of the pitch circle between the centers or other corresponding points of adjacent teeth.

**Circular thickness:** The thickness of the tooth on the pitch circle—also known as arc thickness.

**Clearance:** Radial distance between the top of a tooth and the bottom of the mating tooth space.

**Contact ratio:** Ratio of the arc of action to the circular pitch.

**Dedendum:** Depth of tooth space below pitch circle or radial dimension between the pitch circle and the bottom of a tooth space.

**Diametral pitch:** Ratio of the number of teeth to the number of inches of pitch diameter—equal number of gear teeth to each inch of pitch diameter. (See also normal diametral pitch.)

**Face of tooth:** That surface of the tooth which is between the pitch circle and top of the tooth.

**Face width:** Width of the pitch surface. The active face width is the width which actually makes contact with a mating gear When herringbone gears have a central clearance groove, the width of this groove is not included in the active face width.

**Flank of tooth:** That surface which is between the pitch circle and the bottom land. The flank includes the fillet.

**Internal diameter:** The diameter of a circle coinciding with the tops of the teeth of an internal gear.

**Land:** The **top land** is the top surface of a tooth, and the **bottom land** is the surface of the gear between the flanks of adjacent teeth

**Line of action:** That portion of the common tangent to the base circles along which contact between mating involute gear teeth occurs.

**Module:** Ratio of the pitch diameter to the number of teeth. Ordinarily, module is understood to mean ratio of pitch diameter in millimeters to the number of teeth. The English module is a ratio of the pitch diameter in inches to the number of teeth.

**Normal circular pitch:** The shortest distance on the pitch surface between the centers or any other corresponding points of adjacent teeth—applied to helical gearing.

**Normal diametral pitch:** The diametral pitch corresponding to the normal circular pitch and equal to number of teeth divided by the product of the pitch diameter and the cosine of the helix angle; also equals diametral pitch divided by cosine of the helix angle.

**Normal pressure angle:** Applied to helical gears to indicate pressure angle in a plane normal or perpendicular to the teeth as distinguished from a plane that is perpendicular to the axis of the gear.

**Pitch circle:** A circle the radius of which is equal to the distance from the gear axis to the pitch point.

**Pitch diameter:** Diameter of the pitch circle (generally understood to mean the diameter obtained by dividing the number of teeth by the diametral pitch or the diameter of the pitch circle when the center-to-center distance between mating gears is standard).

**Pitch point:** The point of tangency of the pitch circles or the point where the center-line of mating gears intersects the pitch circles.

**Pressure angle:** The pressure angle of a pair of mating involute gears is the angle between the line of action and a line perpendicular to the center-line of these gears. (See also normal pressure angle.)

**Ratio of gearing:** Ratio of the numbers of teeth on mating gears. Ordinarily the ratio is found by dividing the number of teeth on the larger gear by the number of teeth on the smaller gear or pinion For example, if the ratio is 2 or "2 to 1," this usually means that the smaller gear or pinion makes two revolutions to one revolution of the larger mating gear.

**Root circle:** A circle coinciding with the bottoms of the tooth spaces.

**Root diameter:** Diameter of the root circle.

**Whole depth:** Radial dimension between top of tooth and root circle—also known as total depth.

**Working depth:** Depth to which a tooth extends into the tooth space of a mating gear when the center distance is standard—equals twice the addendum.

both by a regular and simplified method. What is now referred to as the American Standard Pipe thread was formerly known as the National Standard. Dimensions and specifications of pipe threads on drawings are usually made in accordance with the American Standard for Pipe Threads. In indicating threaded sections on drawings it is not necessary to detail the taper unless desired. The pipe thread is generally divided into three sections along its length, that is, the "distance of normal engagement by hand," the "length of the effective thread" and the "imperfect threads." The first of course, refers to the distance you can turn the threaded parts together by hand pressure alone. The second means generally the distance that perfect full-formed threads are cut by the die. The third refers to the section of threads not cut to full depth by the die at the finish end of the thread.

### Thread "Pictures":

When threads are drawn in conventional detail, such as is shown in the upper views, Fig. 32, the representation is often referred to as a thread "picture". In this the helices are shown by slanting straight lines and the thread contour simply indicated as a sharp V. Actually, the helices are slightly curved when viewed from a point at right angles to the axis of the screw and the standard threads are flattened or truncated at the top and spaced at the root.

### Spur Gears:

After a study of the Definitions of Gear Terms and comparing with those for screw threads you can readily see a certain analogy between the two. The spur gear, and also the screw thread, gives a positive means of transmitting power and movement to machine parts, in fact each new development adds to the wide application of the two devices to such purposes. Just as screw threads are of many types, so are gears. We commonly think of bolts and nuts as a means of holding separate parts of an assembly together. Yet that is only one application of the common screw thread. Primarily, the purpose of a spur gear is to provide a positive means of transmitting power and movement from one parallel shaft to another. But that too, is only one application of the spur gear. A pair or a train of spur gears can provide a means of reducing or increasing speed at either a constant or varying rate such as in various types of transmissions. Combinations of gears can be assembled to produce almost any desired system of leverage or of forward and reverse speeds. Normally one thinks of a gear as a round disk or wheel with a given number of teeth cut on its circular face, the teeth being of a size and shape to fit into, or "mesh," with another gear wheel having teeth of like size. The latter wheel may be of the same size (diameter) or it may be larger or smaller as required. But just as we must think of external and internal threads, so we must keep in mind that there are both external and internal spur gears. In the former the minor and major diameters reverse position while in the latter the "addendum" and "dedendum" are in reverse positions. Fig. 33 locates the parts of the spur gear to which the various common terms refer and on the page following you will find the definitions of these and other terms which apply to spur gearing. Fig. 34 shows outlines of American Standard tooth forms for spur gears and the table, Fig. 35, on the following page gives the rules and formulas for determining various dimensions. Fig. 36 shows the manner in which the draftsman ordinarily arranges the working drawing of a spur gear. Here the blank is of such size that it has been cast with arms instead of a center web. As you can see from the revolved section the arms are oval shape, a common form. Only certain of the minor dimensions pertaining to the general size of the blank are given. Fig. 37 gives formulas for proportioning cast spur gears in accordance with requirements for ordinary operating conditions. Gears with arms of oval, ribbed, and H-sections are commonly specified, with the ribbed and H-section arms widely used in large gears. The latter two types of arms reduce weight and at the same time the degree of rigidity is high in proportion to the weight. Incidentally, it may be said that the methods of checking gear sizes are similar to those already described for checking thread sizes, except that two pins of known diameter are used in place of wires.

### Bevel Gears:

Along with the spur gear in which the driving gear turns another on a shaft par-

### American Standard Spur Gear Tooth Forms
(Formulas on next page)

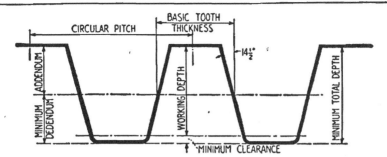

**Basic Rack of the 14 1/2-Degree Full-Depth Involute System**

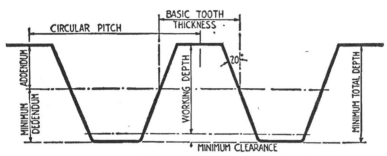

**Basic Rack of the 20-Degree Full-Depth Involute System**

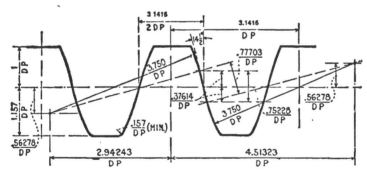

**Approximation of Basic Rack for the 14 1/2-Degree Composite System**

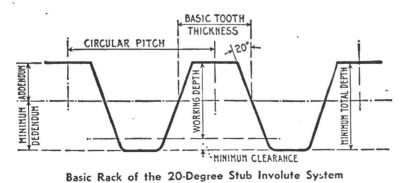

**Basic Rack of the 20-Degree Stub Involute System**

## Fig. 34

### Rules and Formulas for Dimensions of Spur Gears*

| No. of Rule | To Find | Rule | Formula |
|---|---|---|---|
| 1 | Diametral Pitch | Divide 3.1416 by circular pitch. | $P = \dfrac{3.1416}{P'}$ |
| 2 | Circular Pitch | Divide 3.1416 by diametral pitch. | $P' = \dfrac{3.1416}{P}$ |
| 3 | Pitch Diameter | Divide number of teeth by diametral pitch. | $D = \dfrac{N}{P}$ |
| 4 | Pitch Diameter | Multiply number of teeth by circular pitch and divide the product by 3.1416. | $D = \dfrac{NP'}{3.1416}$ |
| 5 | Center Distance | Add the number of teeth in both gears and divide the sum by two times the diametral pitch. | $C = \dfrac{N_g + N_p}{2\,P}$ |
| 6 | Center Distance | Multiply the sum of the number of teeth in both gears by circular pitch and divide the product by 6.2832. | $C = \dfrac{(N_g + N_p)\,P'}{6.2832}$ |
| 7 | Addendum | Divide 1 by diametral pitch. | $S = \dfrac{1}{P}$ |
| 8 | Addendum | Divide circular pitch by 3.1416. | $S = \dfrac{P'}{3.1416}$ |
| 9 | Clearance | Divide 0.157 by diametral pitch. | $\dfrac{0.157}{P}$ |
| 10 | Clearance | Divide circular pitch by 20. | $\dfrac{P'}{20}$ |
| 11 | Whole Depth of Tooth | Divide 2.157 by diametral pitch. | $W = \dfrac{2.157}{P}$ |
| 12 | Whole Depth of Tooth | Multiply 0.6866 by circular pitch. | $W = 0.6866\,P'$ |
| 13 | Thickness of Tooth | Divide 1.5708 by diametral pitch. | $T = \dfrac{1.5708}{P}$ |
| 14 | Thickness of Tooth | Divide circular pitch by 2. | $T = \dfrac{P'}{2}$ |
| 15 | Outside Diameter | Add 2 to the number of teeth and divide the sum by diametral pitch. | $O = \dfrac{N + 2}{P}$ |
| 16 | Outside Diameter | Multiply the sum of the number of teeth plus 2 by circular pitch and divide the product by 3.1416. | $O = \dfrac{(N + 2)\,P'}{3.1416}$ |
| 17 | Diametral Pitch | Divide number of teeth by pitch diameter. | $P = \dfrac{N}{D}$ |
| 18 | Circular Pitch | Multiply pitch diameter by 3.1416 and divide by number of teeth. | $P' = \dfrac{3.1416\,D}{N}$ |
| 19 | Pitch Diameter | Subtract two times the addendum from outside diameter. | $D = O - 2\,S$ |
| 20 | Number of Teeth | Multiply pitch diameter by diametral pitch. | $N = P \times D$ |
| 21 | Number of Teeth | Multiply pitch diameter by 3.1416 and divide the product by circular pitch. | $N = \dfrac{3.1416\,D}{P'}$ |
| 22 | Outside Diameter | Add two times the addendum to the pitch diameter. | $O = D + 2\,S$ |
| 23 | Length of Rack | Multiply number of teeth in rack by 3.1416 and divide by diametral pitch. | $L = \dfrac{3.1416\,N}{P}$ |
| 24 | Length of Rack | Multiply the number of teeth in the rack by circular pitch. | $L = NP'$ |

* Rules and formulas relating to tooth depth and outside diam. apply to full-depth teeth.

## Fig. 35

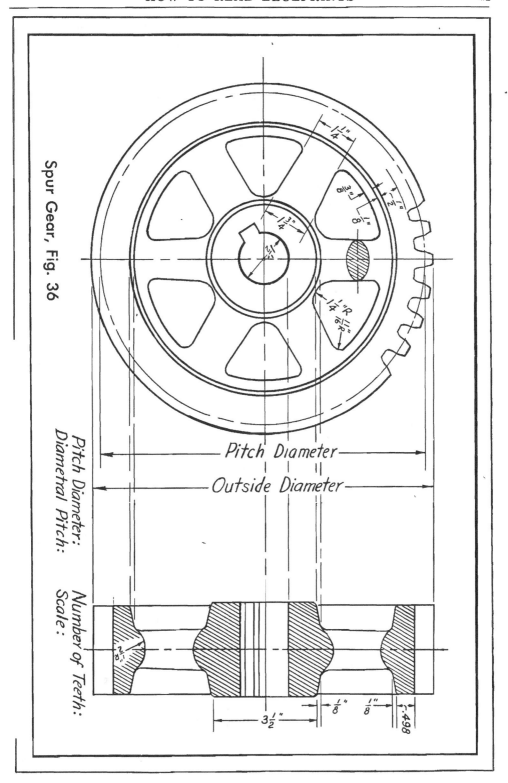

Spur Gear, Fig. 36

Pitch Diameter

Outside Diameter

Pitch Diameter:
Diametral Pitch:

Number of Teeth:
Scale:

## Dimensions of Spur Gears.

### Dimensions of Spur Gears with Oval Arms

**Fig. 37**

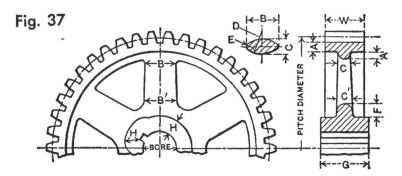

$P$ = diametral pitch, $P'$ = circular pitch.

$A = 1.57 \div P = 0.5\,P'$;     $F = 2.00 \div P = 0.65\,P'$;
$B = 6.28 \div P = 2.0\,P'$;     $G = W + 0.025$ pitch diameter;
$C = 3.14 \div P = P'$;          $H = 0.44 \times$ bore;
$D = 4.71 \div P = 1.5\,P'$;     $B' = B + \frac{3}{4}$ inch per foot;
$E = 0.79 \div P = 0.25\,P'$;    $C' = C + \frac{3}{4}$ inch per foot.

### Dimensions of Spur Gears with Ribbed Arms or Arms of H-section

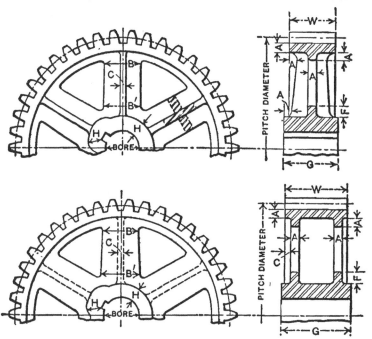

$P$ = diametral pitch, $P'$ = circular pitch.

$A = 1.57 \div P = 0.5\,P'$;     $G = W + 0.025$ pitch diameter;
$B = 7.85 \div P = 2.5\,P'$;     $H = 0.44 \times$ bore;
$C = 0.94 \div P = 0.3\,P'$;     $B' = B + \frac{3}{4}$ inch per foot.
$F = 2.20 \div P = 0.7\,P'$;

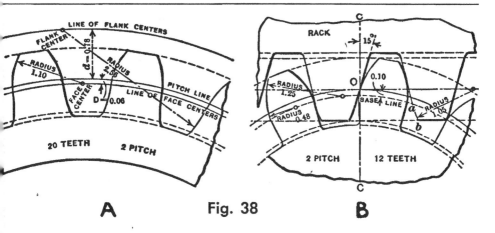

**Fig. 38**

**Special Rule for Involute Rack.** — Draw the sides of the rack teeth as straight lines inclined 15 degrees to the center line *COC*. Draw the outer half *ab* of the face by means of a circular arc having a radii of 2.10 inches divided by the diametral pitch, or 0.67 inch multiplied by the circular pitch, the center for this arc being on the pitch line of the rack.

llel to that on which the driver is mount-d, there are many other types of gear drives. The bevel gear which transmits power to shafts at right angles, or "around a corner" so to speak, the worm gear in which the driver is in a sense a screw, and he many types of spiral gearing which can be designed to drive shafts positioned at most any angle desired. Because the teeth, when engaging, strike full-tooth contact simultaneously, the spur and bevel gear drives are more or less noisy under heavy loads at the higher speeds. And variations in the load at a given speed tend to aggravate this objectionable condition. Hence, with the introduction of high-speed drives carrying relatively heavy loads designers and engineers have developed and refined the various forms of spiral gearing, the spiral bevel gear, and the hypoid gear. The latter is essentially a form of spiral-bevel gear except that the axis of the driving pinion is offset in relation to the axis of the driven gear. In all these latter gears there is a continuous contact of the teeth at the pitch line. And instead of a fixed, simultaneous contact along the whole length of only one tooth on each gear, as is the case with spur gears, there is a sliding contact involving a number of teeth at any given time. This action distributes the load over a greater area, thus reducing wear and en-

abling the spiral gear to operate quietly under heavy loads at high speeds. This latter feature of the spiral gear is also due in large part to the progressive engagement of the teeth which results in a more gradual transmission of the load from one tooth surface to another. This continuous "loading" and "unloading" of the teeth in a gradual and uniform sequence, the smoothness of which suggests a "wiping" or "camming" action, enables gears of this type to stand up under heavy "shock" loads such as occur in truck and tractor operation, for example. When the object is high efficiency in power transmission and absolute silence and smoothness of operation, as in rear axle drives of automobiles and trucks the hypoid gear is generally used. In this gear the position of the pinion below the center of the driven gear results in a somewhat shorter lengthwise sliding of the teeth by one another. This tends to reduce frictional loss, or "parasitic" drag as it is sometimes termed, even further. And due to the offset of the gear axes which allows the shafts to extend by one another, the bearing-mounting problems are greatly simplified. Because of these features the hypoid gear operates even more silently and smoothly than the spiral bevel gear under varying loads and speeds.

## Grant's Odontograph

### Table for Cycloidal Teeth

| Number of Teeth in the Gear | | $R, r, D$ and $d$ for One Diametral Pitch; for any other Pitch divide Values given by that Pitch | | | | $R, D$ and $d$ for One Inch Circular Pitch; for any other Pitch multiply Values given by that Pitch | | | |
|---|---|---|---|---|---|---|---|---|---|
| | | Faces | | Flanks | | Faces | | Flanks | |
| Exact | Also Used for | $R$ | $D$ | $r$ | $d$ | $R$ | $D$ | $r$ | $d$ |
| 10 | 10 | 1.99 | 0.02 | −8.00 | 4.00 | 0.62 | 0.01 | −2.55 | 1.27 |
| 11 | 11 | 2.00 | 0.04 | −11.05 | 6.50 | 0.63 | 0 01 | −3.34 | 2.07 |
| 12 | 12 | 2.01 | 0.06 | ∞ | ∞ | 0.64 | 0.02 | ∞ | ∞ |
| 13½ | 13- 14 | 2.04 | 0.07 | 15.10 | 9.43 | 0.65 | 0.02 | 4.80 | 3.00 |
| 15½ | 15- 16 | 2.10 | 0.09 | 7.86 | 3.46 | 0.67 | 0.03 | 2.50 | 1.10 |
| 17½ | 17- 18 | 2.14 | 0.11 | 6.13 | 2.20 | 0.68 | 0 04 | 1.95 | 0.70 |
| 20 | 19- 21 | 2.20 | 0.13 | 5 12 | 1.57- | 0.70 | 0 04 | 1.63 | 0.50 |
| 23 | 22- 24 | 2.26 | 0.15 | 4.50 | 1.13 | 0.72 | 0.05 | 1.43 | 0.36 |
| 27 | 25- 29 | 2.33 | 0 16 | 4.10 | 0.96 | 0.74 | 0 05 | 1.30 | 0.29 |
| 33 | 30- 36 | 2.40 | 0.19 | 3.80 | 0.72 | 0.76 | 0.06 | 1.20 | 0.23 |
| 42 | 37- 48 | 2.48 | 0.22 | 3.52 | 0.63 | 0.79 | 0 07 | 1.12 | 0.20 |
| 58 | 49- 72 | 2.60 | 0 25 | 3.33 | 0.54 | 0 83 | 0.08 | 1.06 | 0.17 |
| 97 | 73-144 | 2.83 | 0.28 | 3.14 | 0.44 | 0.90 | 0.09 | 1.00 | 0.14 |
| 290 | 145-300 | 2.92 | 0.31 | 3.00 | 0.38 | 0 93 | 0.10 | 0.95 | 0.12 |
| ∞ | Rack | 2 96 | 0.34 | 2.96 | 0.34 | 0.94 | 0.11 | 0.94 | 0 11 |

### Table for Involute Teeth

| No. of Teeth in the Gear | Radii for One Diametral Pitch; for any other Pitch divide Values given by that Pitch | | Radii for One Inch Circular Pitch; for any other Pitch multiply Values given by that Pitch | | No. of Teeth in the Gear | Radii for One Diametral Pitch; for any other Pitch divide Values given by that Pitch | | Radii for One Inch Circular Pitch; for any other Pitch multiply Values given by that Pitch | |
|---|---|---|---|---|---|---|---|---|---|
| | Face Radius | Flank Radius | Face Radius | Flank Radius | | Face Radius | Flank Radius | Face Radius | Flank Radius |
| 10 | 2.28 | 0.69 | 0 73 | 0 22 | 28 | 3.92 | 2 59 | 1 25 | 0 82 |
| 11 | 2.40 | 0.83 | 0.76 | 0.27 | 29 | 3.99 | 2 67 | 1 27 | 0 85 |
| 12 | 2.51 | 0 96 | 0.80 | 0.31 | 30 | 4.06 | 2 76 | 1 29 | 0 88 |
| 13 | 2.62 | 1.09 | 0.83 | 0.34 | 31 | 4.13 | 2 85 | 1.31 | 0.91 |
| 14 | 2.72 | 1.22 | 0.87 | 0.39 | 32 | 4.20 | 2 93 | 1 34 | 0 93 |
| 15 | 2.82 | 1.34 | 0 90 | 0 43 | 33 | 4.27 | 3 01 | 1.36 | 0.96 |
| 16 | 2.92 | 1.46 | 0 93 | 0 47 | 34 | 4 33 | 3.09 | 1.38 | 0.99 |
| 17 | 3.02 | 1.58 | 0 96 | 0.50 | 35 | 4 39 | 3 16 | 1.39 | 1 01 |
| 18 | 3.12 | 1 69 | 0 99 | 0.54 | 36 | 4 45 | 3 23 | 1 41 | 1.03 |
| 19 | 3.22 | 1.79 | 1.03 | 0.57 | 37- 40 | 4 20 | | 1.34 | |
| 20 | 3.32 | 1.89 | 1.06 | 0 60 | 41- 45 | 4 63 | | 1.48 | |
| 21 | 3.41 | 1.98 | 1.09 | 0 63 | 46- 51 | 5 06 | | 1.61 | |
| 22 | 3.49 | 2.06 | 1.11 | 0.66 | 52- 60 | 5.74 | | 1.83 | |
| 23 | 3.57 | 2.15 | 1.13 | 0 69 | 61- 70 | 6 52 | | 2.07 | |
| 24 | 3.64 | 2.24 | 1.16 | 0.71 | 71- 90 | 7.72 | | 2.46 | |
| 25 | 3.71 | 2.33 | 1.18 | 0.74 | 91-120 | 9.78 | | 3.11 | |
| 26 | 3.78 | 2.42 | 1.20 | 0 77 | 121-180 | 13 38 | | 4.26 | |
| 27 | 3 85 | 2.50 | 1.23 | 0 80 | 181-360 | 21.62 | | 6.88 | |

Fig. 39

$N$ = number of teeth;

$P$ = diametral pitch;

$P'$ = circular pitch;

$\pi$ = 3.1416;

$\alpha$ = pitch cone angle and edge angle;

$\gamma$ = center angle;

$D$ = pitch diameter;

$S$ = addendum;

$S+A$ = dedendum ($A$ = clearance);

$W$ = whole depth of tooth space;

$T$ = thickness of tooth at pitch line;

$C$ = pitch cone radius;

$F$ = width of face;

$s$ = addendum at small end of tooth;

$t$ = thickness of tooth at pitch line at small end;

$\theta$ = addendum angle;

$\phi$ = dedendum angle;

$\delta$ = face angle;

$\zeta$ = cutting angle;

$K$ = angular addendum;

$O$ = outside diameter (edge diameter for internal gears);

$J$ = vertex distance;

$j$ = vertex distance at small end;

$N'$ = number of teeth for which to select cutter, also called "number of teeth in equivalent spur gear."

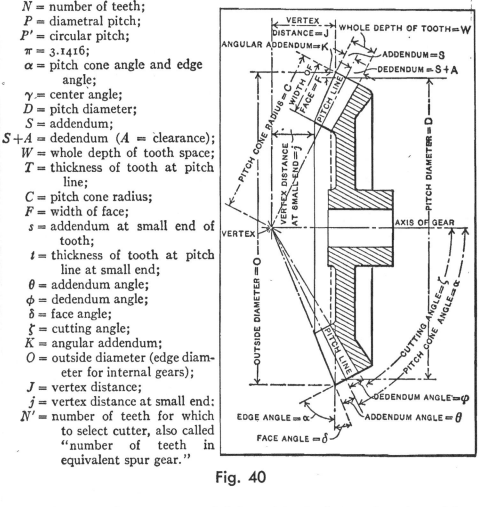

Fig. 40

The table, Fig. 39, known as it is titled, "Grants' Odontograph", gives the values for laying out gear teeth by simply striking circular arcs. Fig. 38 gives typical examples for both the cycloidal, A, and the involute systems, B. The arcs, if laid out in accordance with the values given in the tables, result in a very close approximation of the tooth curves. To follow through with the table of the cycloidal system the draftsman first, proceeds with the pitch, root, addendum, and clearance circles in the regular way. Then outside these he draws the circle entitled "line of flank centers", Fig. 38, A, at the distance d, the latter value being taken from the table. Then he draws the "line of face centers" inside the pitch line, the value D in the table determining its distance from the pitch line. Then he sets the dividers to the radius R, taken from the table, and draws in the face curves; and then finally the flank curves with the radius r from centers on the line of flank centers previously drawn. This results in the series of reverse curves which outline the gear teeth as you see them in Fig. 38, A. It should be noted from the table in Fig. 39, the cycloidal system, that the values pertaining to pitches are for 1 diametral and 1 inch circular pitch only and that for any other pitch one must either divide or multiply as directed.

Using the table for the involute system the draftsman again draws the pitch, addendum, root, and clearance circles in the regular way. Then he draws a base line

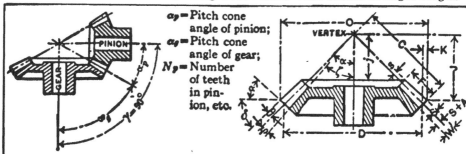

$\alpha_p =$ Pitch cone angle of pinion;
$\alpha_g =$ Pitch cone angle of gear;
$N_p =$ Number of teeth in pinion, etc.

Use Rules and Formulas Nos. 1 to 21 in the order given.

| No. | To Find | | Rule | Formula |
|---|---|---|---|---|
| 1 | | Pitch Cone Angle (or Edge Angle) of Pinion. | Divide the number of teeth in the pinion by the number of teeth in the gear to get the tangent. | $\tan \alpha_p = \dfrac{N_p}{N_g}$ |
| 2 | | Pitch Cone Angle (or Edge Angle) of Gear. | Divide the number of teeth in the gear by the number of teeth in the pinion to get the tangent. | $\tan \alpha_g = \dfrac{N_g}{N_p}$ |
| 3 | | Proof of Calculations for Pitch Cone Angles. | The sum of the pitch cone angles of the pinion and gear equals 90 degrees. | $\alpha_p + \alpha_g = 90°$ |
| 4 | | Pitch Diameter. | Divide the number of teeth by the diametral pitch; or multiply the number of teeth by the circular pitch and divide by 3.1416. | $D = \dfrac{N}{P} = \dfrac{NP'}{\pi}$ |
| 5 | These dimensions are the same for both gear and pinion. | Addendum. | Divide 1.0 by the diametral pitch; or multiply the circular pitch by 0.318. | $S = \dfrac{1.0}{P}$ $= 0.318\,P'$ |
| 6 | | Dedendum. | Divide 1.157 by the diametral pitch; or multiply the circular pitch by 0.368. | $S + A = \dfrac{1.157}{P}$ $= 0.368\,P'$ |
| 7 | | Whole Depth of Tooth Space. | Divide 2.157 by the diametral pitch; or multiply the circular pitch by 0.687. | $W = \dfrac{2.157}{P}$ $= 0.687\,P'$ |
| 8 | | Thickness of Tooth at Pitch Line. | Divide 1.571 by the diametral pitch; or divide the circular pitch by 2. | $T = \dfrac{1.571}{P} = \dfrac{P'}{2}$ |
| 9 | | Pitch Cone Radius. | Divide the pitch diameter by twice the sine of the pitch cone angle. | $C = \dfrac{D}{2 \times \sin \alpha}$ |
| 10 | | Addendum of Small End of Tooth. | Subtract the width of face from the pitch cone radius, divide the remainder by the pitch cone radius and multiply by the addendum. | $s = S \times \dfrac{C - F}{C}$ |
| 11 | | Thickness of Tooth at Pitch Line at Small End. | Subtract the width of face from the pitch cone radius, divide the remainder by the pitch cone radius and multiply by the thickness of the tooth at the pitch line. | $t = T \times \dfrac{C - F}{C}$ |
| 12 | | Addendum Angle. | Divide the addendum by the pitch cone radius to get the tangent. | $\tan \theta = \dfrac{S}{C}$ |
| 13 | | Dedendum Angle. | Divide the dedendum by the pitch cone radius to get the tangent. | $\tan \phi = \dfrac{S + 1}{C}$ |

Fig. 41

### Rules and Formulas for Calculating Bevel Gears with Shafts at Right Angles

| No. | To Find | Rule | Formula |
|---|---|---|---|
| 14 | Face Angle. | Subtract the sum of the pitch cone and addendum angles from 90 degrees. | $\delta = 90° - (\alpha + \theta)$ |
| 15 | Cutting Angle.* | Subtract the dedendum angle from the pitch cone angle | $\zeta = \alpha - \phi$ |
| 16 | Angular Addendum. | Multiply the addendum by the cosine of the pitch cone angle. | $K = S \times \cos \alpha$ |
| 17 | Outside Diameter. | Add twice the angular addendum to the pitch diameter. | $O = D + 2K$ |
| 18 | Apex Distance. | Multiply one-half the outside diameter by the tangent of the face angle. | $J = \dfrac{O}{2} \times \tan \delta$ |
| 19 | Apex Distance at Small End of Tooth. | Subtract the width of face from the pitch cone radius; divide the remainder by the pitch cone radius and multiply by the apex distance. | $j = J \times \dfrac{C - F}{C}$ |
| 20 | Number of Teeth for which to Select Cutter. | Divide the number of teeth by the cosine of the pitch cone angle. | $N' = \dfrac{N}{\cos \alpha}$ |
| 21 | Proof of Calculations by Rules Nos. 9, 12, 14, 16 and 17. | The outside diameter equals twice the pitch cone radius multiplied by the cosine of the face angle and divided by the cosine of the addendum angle. | $O = \dfrac{2C \times \cos \delta}{\cos \theta}$ |

## Fig. 41, continued

⅟₆₀ of the pitch diameter inside the pitch line. Using the face radius values given in the table he draws in the tooth faces from the pitch line to the addendum line, with the centers on the base line previously drawn. Again from the table he gets the flank radius for drawing the flanks of the teeth from the pitch line to the base line, the centers being on the base line, of course. Then finally he extends the flanks with straight radial lines from the base line to the root line and rounds these into the clearance line. See Fig. 38, B.

**Formulas for Bevel Gear Calculations:**

In Figs. 40 and 41 are given the rules and formulas and the symbols used in formulas for the calculation of bevel gears with shafts at a right angle. The numbers given in the left-hand column, Fig. 41, are for convenient reference to any particular rule. The rules and formulas are given in the order in which they would ordinarily be used by the designer of bevel gearing. The names of the various angles and dimensions referred to in bevel gearing are given in the drawing at the right, Fig. 40. The notation used in the formulas, Fig. 41, is easily understood by comparing the formula with the corresponding rule. Symbols and the parts to which they refer are shown at the left in Fig. 40.

The following exception to the rules given should be noted:

The Brown & Sharpe Mfg. Co. recommends that for shaping bevel gear teeth with a formed cutter, the cutting angle be determined by subtracting the addendum angle from the pitch cone angle, instead of subtracting the dedendum angle, as in Rule 15. In other words, the clearance at the bottom of the tooth is made uniform instead of tapering toward the vertex. This gives a somewhat closer approximation to the desired shape.*

It should be kept in mind that while Fig. 41 gives only rules and formulas for calculating bevel gears with shafts at right angles, bevel gears are also mounted with shafts in other positions, as at an acute

---

* Text on formulas for bevel gear calculations reprinted from Machinery's Handbook by courtesy of the publishers.

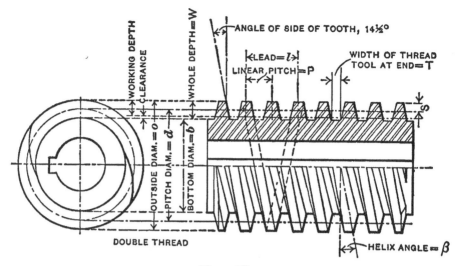

Fig. 42

$P$ = circular pitch of wheel and linear pitch of worm;

$l$ = lead of worm;

$n$ = number of teeth or threads in worm;

$S$ = addendum, or height of worm tooth above pitch line;

$d$ = pitch diameter of worm;

$D$ = pitch diameter of worm-wheel;

$o$ = outside diameter of worm;

$O$ = throat diameter of worm-wheel;

$O'$ = outside diameter of worm-wheel (to sharp corners);

$b$ = bottom or root diameter of worm;

$N$ = number of teeth in worm-wheel;

$W$ = whole depth of worm tooth;

$T$ = width of thread tool at end;

$\alpha$ = face angle of worm-wheel;

$\beta$ = helix angle of worm and gashing angle of wheel;

$U$ = radius of curvature of worm-wheel throat;

$C$ = distance between centers;

$x$ = threaded length of worm.

---

angle and an obtuse angle. There are also several types which come under the general classification of bevel gears, such as crown gears, and internal bevel gears. The latter are rarely used in high-speed machinery due to the great difficulty of cutting the teeth. Hence they are generally furnished only in the rough casting and are used for slow-speed applications where tooth precision is not important and where their characteristics make them of particular advantage in certain types of drives.

In all drives using bevel gears, spiral-bevel gears, in general all angle drives involving the use of gears, special attention must be given to bearing loads, bearing mountings, and the type of bearings used. In ordinary bevel gearing, for example, end play in the shafts, either one or both, causes the driving gear to "climb" the teeth of the driven gear and the "wedging" pressure resulting from this condition tends to bend the shaft of the driving gear out of aline-ment laterally and causes the teeth to take the driving pressure nearer the outer end, greatly accelerating wear and increasing the chance of breakage and "stripping". In the spiral bevel, hypoid, and the many forms of spiral-gear drives the torque or driving force sets up both radial and lateral thrusts which must be taken by the bearing, without movement in either direction. This means that in these gears the pinion should be mounted in either double-row ball bearings of a type capable of carrying both thrust and radial loads, or

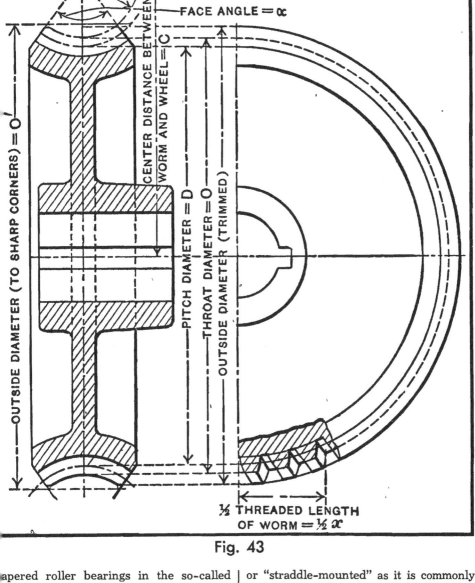

Fig. 43

apered roller bearings in the so-called "indirect" mounting. In the latter each bearing is located in a mounting back of the pinion with the small ends of the tapered rollers to the inside. In this way the bearings carry the radial load equally and at the same time take care of end thrust in both directions. Often in automobile, truck and tractor rear-axle assemblies the spiral pinion is placed between bearings, or "straddle-mounted" as it is commonly termed. Here the two tapered roller bearings are placed as described and in addition a projection of the shaft beyond the small end of the pinion is carried in a straight roller bearing. In all such drives both pinion and gear must be provided with bearings which "lock" against thrust in either direction. The best practice always requires that spiral and spiral bevel

## Rules and Formulas for Worm Gearing

| No. | To Find | Rule | Formula |
|---|---|---|---|
| 1 | Linear Pitch. | Divide the lead by the number of threads. — It is understood that by the number of threads is meant, not number of threads per inch, but the number of threads in the whole worm — one, if it is single-threaded, four, if it is quadruple-threaded, etc. | $P = \dfrac{l}{n}$ |
| 2 | Addendum of Worm Tooth. | Multiply the linear pitch by 0.3183. | $S = 0.3183\,P$ |
| 3 | Pitch Diameter of Worm. | Subtract twice the addendum from the outside diameter. | $d = o - 2\,S$ |
| 4 | Pitch Diameter of Worm-wheel. | Multiply the number of teeth in the wheel by the linear pitch of the worm, and divide the product by 3.1416. | $D = \dfrac{NP}{3.1416}$ |
| 5 | Center Distance between Worm and Gear. | Add together the pitch diameter of the worm and the pitch diameter of the worm-wheel, and divide the sum by 2. | $C = \dfrac{D + d}{2}$ |
| 6 | Whole Depth of Worm Tooth | Multiply the linear pitch by 0.6866. | $W = 0.6866\,P$ |
| 7 | Bottom Diameter of Worm. | Subtract twice the whole depth of tooth from the outside diameter. | $b = o - 2\,W$ |
| 8 | Helix Angle of Worm. | Multiply the pitch diameter of the worm by 3.1416, and divide the product by the lead; the quotient is the cotangent of the helix angle of the worm. | $\cot \beta = \dfrac{3.1416\,d}{l}$ |
| 9 | Width of Thread Tool at End. | Multiply the linear pitch by 0.31. | $T = 0.31\,P$ |
| 10 | Throat Diameter of Worm-wheel. | Add twice the addendum of the worm tooth to the pitch diameter of the worm-wheel. | $O = D + 2\,S$ |
| 11 | Radius of Worm-wheel Throat. | Subtract twice the addendum of the worm tooth from half the outside diameter of the worm. | $U = \dfrac{o}{2} - 2\,S$ |
| 12 | Diameter of Worm-wheel to Sharp Corners. See also Rim Shape and Formulas on page 751. | Multiply the radius of curvature of the worm-wheel throat by the cosine of half the face angle, subtract this quantity from the radius of curvature, multiply the remainder by 2, and add the product to the throat diameter of the worm-wheel. | $O' = 2\left( U - U \times \cos \dfrac{\alpha}{2} \right) + O$ |
| 13 | Minimum Length of Worm for Complete Action. | Multiply 8 times the pitch diameter of the worm-wheel by the addendum; the square root of this product equals the minimum length of worm. | $x = \sqrt{8\,DS}$ |
| 14 | Outside Diameter of Worm. | Add together the pitch diameter and twice the addendum. | $o = d + 2\,S$ |
| 15 | Pitch Diameter of Worm. | Subtract the pitch diameter of the worm-wheel from twice the center distance. | $d = 2\,C - D$ |

## Fig. 44

gears of the many types be mounted in an oil-tight housing so that the parts are supplied with adequate lubrication at all times.

## Worm Gearing:

Worm gearing is quite generally used as a positive drive where extraordinary speed or velocity reduction is required. Worm gears frequently will be found where there are unusually heavy initial loads, that is, starting loads. Some high-ratio worm gears are "self-locking", that is, the frictional coefficients are such that the worm wheel or sector cannot rotate the worm should there be pressure or impact on the wheel or sector which would tend to rotate it in the opposite direction. Certain types of steering gears are one application of this type of worm gear. It should be noted, however, that worm gears with the self-locking feature are not adapted to continuous drives due to comparatively low efficiency. Figs. 42 and 43 give the common nomenclature of both the worm and worm wheel and the rules and formulas for calculating worm gearing are given in Fig. 44. It sometimes happens that design requirements make it necessary to make certain departures from the rules, particularly when the worm wheel is to have a small number of teeth.

Space is not available here to go into all the data in connection with the many forms of gear drives. Only those in most common use have been mentioned. Hence it is suggested that to further his knowledge of gear data and applications, the student obtain a Machinist's Handbook in which he will find the subject of gearing fully covered in a comprehensive and helpful manner. In connection with study of subjects closely interrelated to blueprint reading it may be said that knowledge is simply a word synonym for security and that a study of the initial subject of blueprint reading is a basis for future education and advancement in any of the machine trades.

## Reading Working Drawings:

It will be recalled that we have mentioned working drawings before only in connection with elemental principles. Now there comes the opportunity to study reproductions of several working drawings which have actually been used in the shop in making up machine parts. Take the first one dimensioning the Grinder Body, Fig.

45, as an example. The print is typical of those quite commonly used in production shops in that it carries an identifying number, placed so that it is easily located in a file, and also a running specification on limit dimensions which have been adopted as standard for the plant and the type and nature of the work being done.

Now let's assume for a moment that we are in the shop and are looking over the print to get in mind the essential information and specifications it contains relative to the machine operations on the part which is detailed. Looking first at the title box in the lower right-hand corner we note three facts first off: That the part is a unit of a key-numbered assembly, that the material is cast iron and the scale is full size. Looking at the details we can see the familiar top, side, and end views and also a sectional view taken along the line A-A shown in the top view. Further, in the sectional view A-A, the draftsman has included a top and bottom view of the tapped hole, these two views giving the locating data. Connecting section A-A with the side view we can see that the draftsman has specified the tap size and the body drill size and depth in notes. Close examination of the top and side views turns up two holes at right angles which intersect through a portion of their diameters within the body of the casting. Noting that there is only the single ream dimension for both, we assume, of course, that these holes are cored through the casting and that they are so placed for the purpose of fitting some type of cam locking device. The finish mark "f" appears on certain surfaces in the top and end views and if we connect the finish marks with certain of the dimensions given we can see at once that two of the inside diameters are to be finished to very close limits, the tolerance being .0005, five ten-thousandths of an inch, in fact. One dimension in the sectional end view is specified as "Turn", which usually means a lathe finish, within limits of .001 inch, while the inside diameter is specified as "Ream", within a limit of .0005 in. The sectional end view incidentally, is an example of how sectional views can be used as a "convenience", for in this instance the view enables the draftsman to show the critical dimensions more clearly. Notice too, that all tap and hole sizes are given as notes.

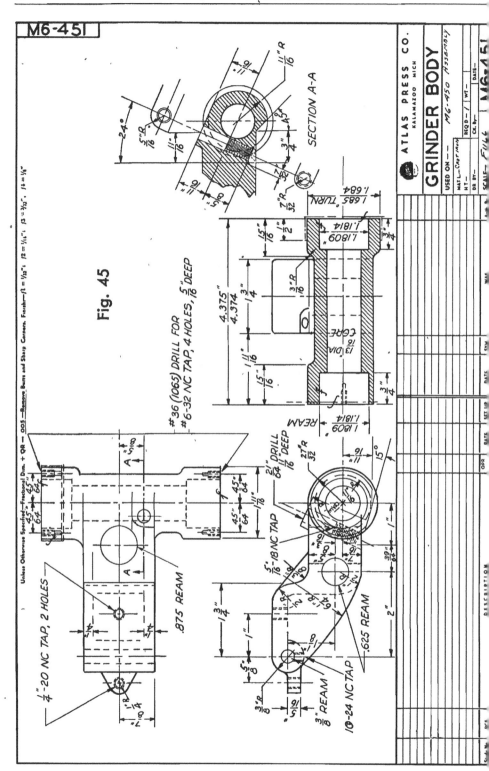

Fig. 45

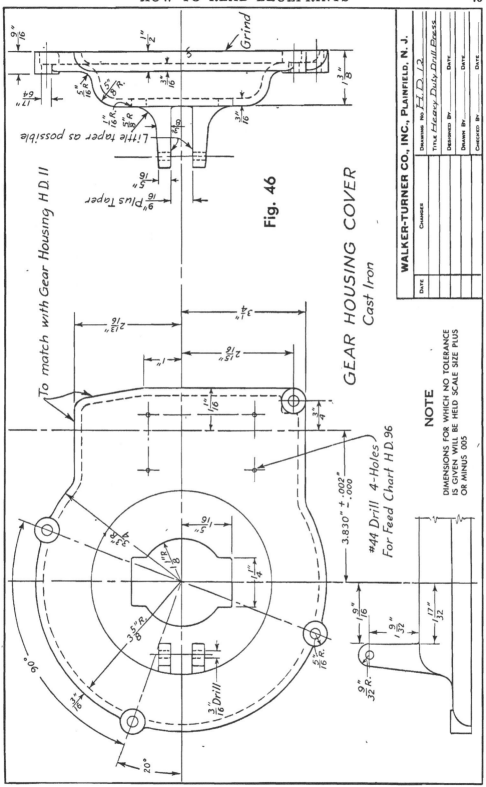

Fig. 46

GEAR HOUSING COVER
Cast Iron

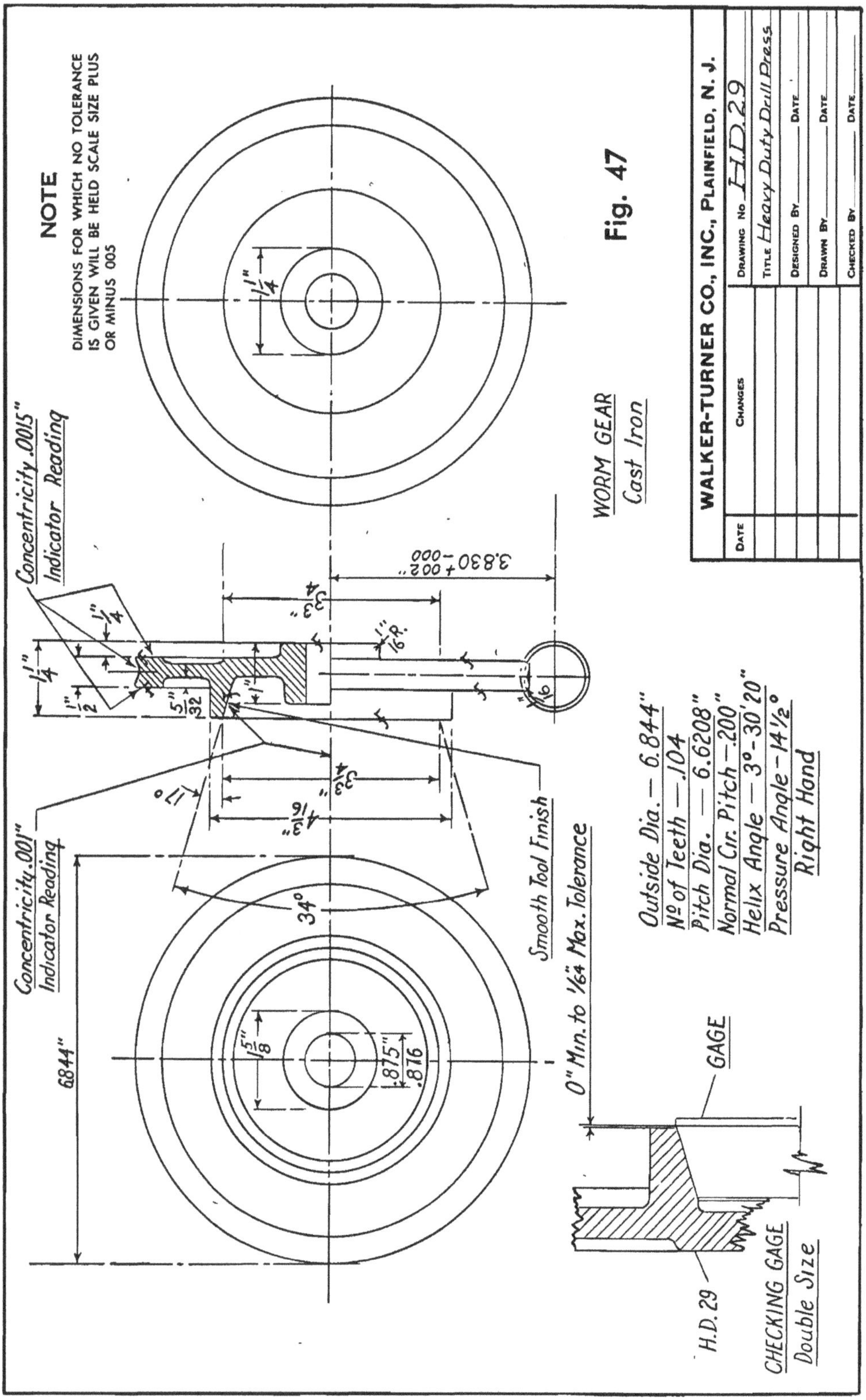

**NOTE**

DIMENSIONS FOR WHICH NO TOLERANCE IS GIVEN WILL BE HELD SCALE SIZE PLUS OR MINUS .005

$\frac{1}{4}$"

WORM GEAR
Cast Iron

**Fig. 47**

Concentricity .0015"
Indicator Reading

Concentricity .001"
Indicator Reading

$3.830 ^{+.002}_{-.000}$"

$\frac{3}{4}$"

$\frac{1}{4}$"

$\frac{1}{2}$"

$\frac{1}{4}$"

$\frac{5}{32}$"

$\frac{1}{16}$"R.

$\frac{1}{9}$"

$\frac{3}{4}$"

$\frac{3}{16}$"

17°

34°

6.844"

$\frac{5}{8}$"

.875
.816

Smooth Tool Finish

0" Min. to $\frac{1}{64}$" Max. Tolerance

Outside Dia. — 6.844"
Nº of Teeth — .104
Pitch Dia. — 6.6208"
Normal Cir. Pitch — .200"
Helix Angle – 3° – 30' 20"
Pressure Angle – 14½°
Right Hand

GAGE

H.D. 29

CHECKING GAGE
Double Size

WALKER-TURNER CO., INC., PLAINFIELD, N. J.

DRAWING No H.D.29
TITLE Heavy Duty Drill Press
DESIGNED BY _____ DATE _____
DRAWN BY _____ DATE _____
CHECKED BY _____ DATE _____

DATE    CHANGES

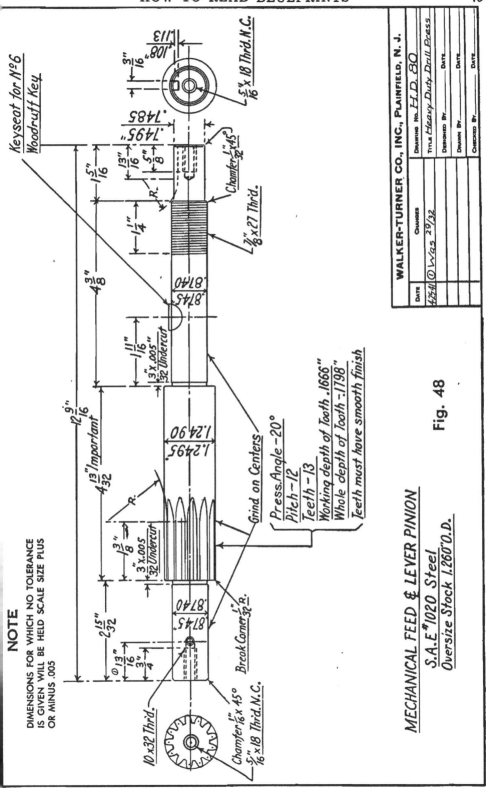

## NOTE

DIMENSIONS FOR WHICH NO TOLERANCE IS GIVEN WILL BE HELD SCALE SIZE PLUS OR MINUS .005

**WALKER-TURNER CO., INC., PLAINFIELD, N. J.**

DRAWING NO. *H.D. 80*

TITLE *Heavy Duty Drill Press*

DESIGNED BY _____ DATE _____

DRAWN BY _____ DATE _____

CHECKED BY _____ DATE _____

| DATE | CHANGES |
|---|---|
| 4-25-41 | ① W as 29/32 |

**Fig. 48**

## MECHANICAL FEED & LEVER PINION

*S.A.E.#1020 Steel*
*Oversize Stock 1.260"O.D.*

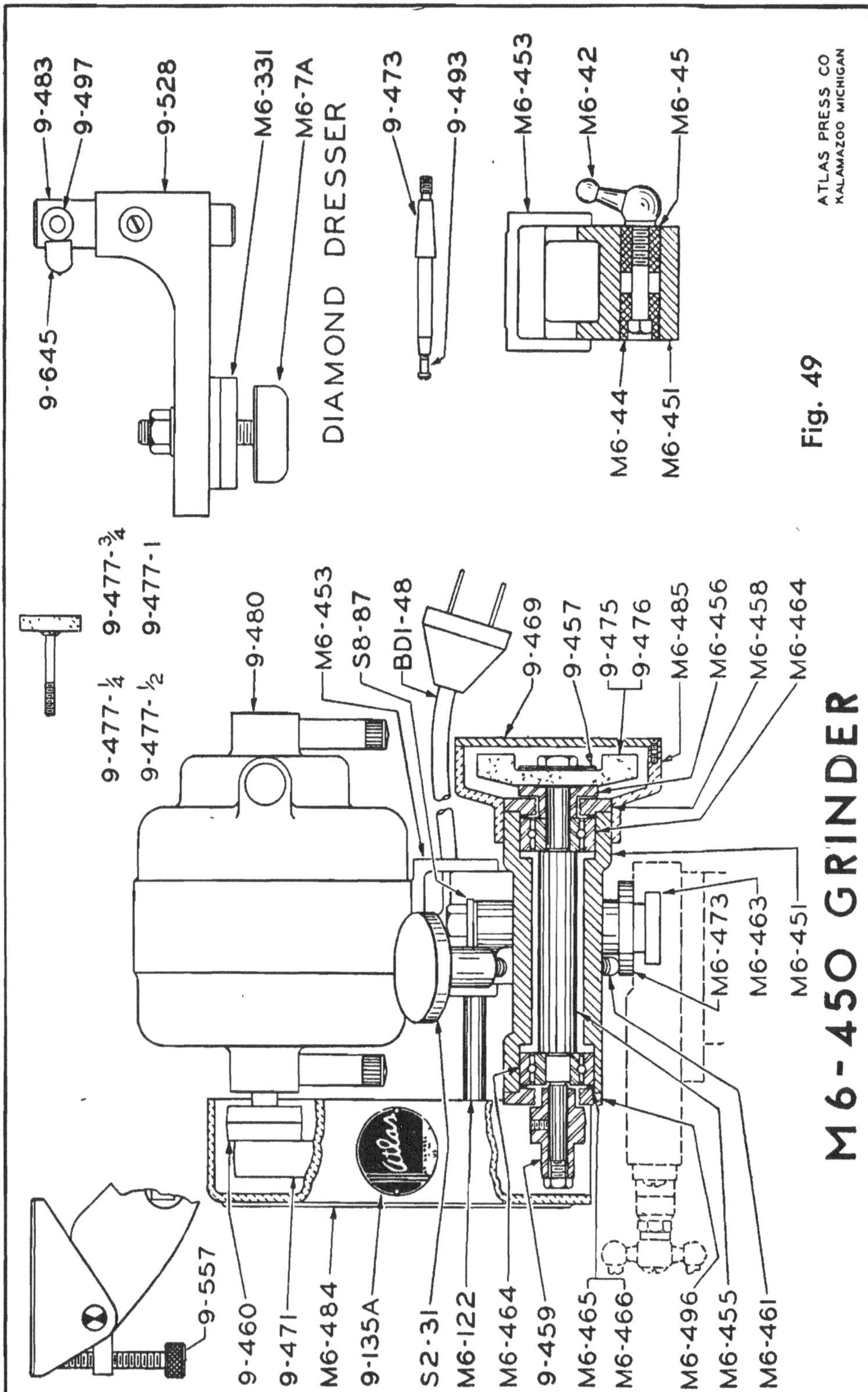

DIAMOND DRESSER

9-483
9-497
9-528
M6-331
M6-7A
9-645
9-473
9-493
M6-453
M6-42
M6-45
M6-44
M6-451

ATLAS PRESS CO
KALAMAZOO MICHIGAN

Fig. 49

9-477-¾
9-477-1
9-477-¼
9-477-½
9-480
M6-453
S8-87
BDI-48
9-469
9-457
9-475
9-476
M6-485
M6-456
M6-458
M6-464
M6-473
M6-463
M6-451

9-557
9-460
9-471
M6-484
9-135A
S2-31
M6-122
M6-464
9-459
M6-465
M6-466
M6-496
M6-455
M6-461

# M6-450 GRINDER

Fig. 46 brings up essentially the same type of "shop" print, but detailing a different object. From a note on the drawing we know at once that this part matches with another in at least a portion of its outline. We know from the tolerance dimension that the distance between the two parallel center lines is important, and although here only two fractional dimensions are set off from the right center line, an experienced machinist would immediately conclude that this is a part of a housing for a worm gear. And he also would conclude that inasmuch as only one drilling specification is given, that for the remaining holes is included on another print, probably that of the matching housing. In the end view one finish mark "f" appears along with the specification "Grind" which means that the whole face of the casting is to be finished flat to form an oil-tight joint with the housing. Fig. 47 is a good example of how the draftsman makes up a drawing on gearing, in this case a worm wheel. Data for milling or hobbing the gear teeth is given in a note. Notice that there are two indicator readings specified. These mean in this case that the surfaces referred to shall not check more than the specified dimension out of round. And finally by referring to Fig. 46 we can see that the limit dimension on the horizontal center lines checks with the dimension on the vertical center lines in Fig. 47. And as the titles are the same we know that these prints are two of a series on the same machine. If we look further at Fig. 48 we can see that this latter print is a third in the same series. The next thing noticed in the title box, Fig. 48, is that a dimension has been changed and looking at the left end of the shaft or spindle we find the reference number "1" and the dimension $13\frac{3}{16}$ in. In this case the pinion is integral and the spindle is machined to four diameters, each of which is dimensioned with tolerances written in decimals reading to four places. This means, of course, that these diameters must be held within very close limits. Notice the radius symbol "R" at the right end of the shaft and also at the finish end of the pinion teeth. In the first instance this means that the key-way cutter is to run its full depth and width for a distance of $13\frac{3}{16}$ in. and then finish with its own radius. Essentially the same is true of the second symbol. One dimension is especially emphasized with the word, "Important". We can assume either that it is important in itself or because it takes precedence over another registering dimension in some other unit of an assembly of which the pinion is a part. However, the concern of the blueprint reader and also the machinist is usually only with the print in hand. It is his business to correctly interpret the information on the print and do the work specified. As can be seen from the three prints we have just reviewed in general, the necessity for visualization of a complete machine and the location of its component parts is mostly eliminated. From this, however, the student should not gain the impression that the ability to visualize need not be cultivated. Every drawing presents its own problems to the blueprint reader and machinist. And acquiring a background of knowledge of the common machine parts, their general appearance, characteristics and assemblies into working units is essential to quick and accurate interpretation of blueprints.

## Assembly Drawings:

Working drawings show dimensioned parts of machines, as we have already learned. They show the parts separately and detail each one individually. The assembly drawing shows where these parts go and what relation they bear to each other. The assembly drawing gives more nearly a "picture" of the completed machine. It may consist of only one or several views and as its purpose is to show where and how all principal parts fit, these may be full views, sectional views and cutaway views—whatever is necessary to show complete assembly of the machine or unit. Occasionally, although not so frequently in drawings of machines, the draftsman will resort to a perspective drawing showing the unit "taken apart," that is, a view looking inside, also sometimes called an "exploded" view.

Fig. 49 is one example of an assembly drawing. If you study it closely you will see that the "grinder-body" detailed in the working drawing, Fig. 45, is a part of the assembly view, Fig. 49. The note in the title box, Fig. 45, indicates that the part No. M6-451 is used on the No. M6-450 assembly as shown in Fig. 49. As you see from the latter the parts are all key num-

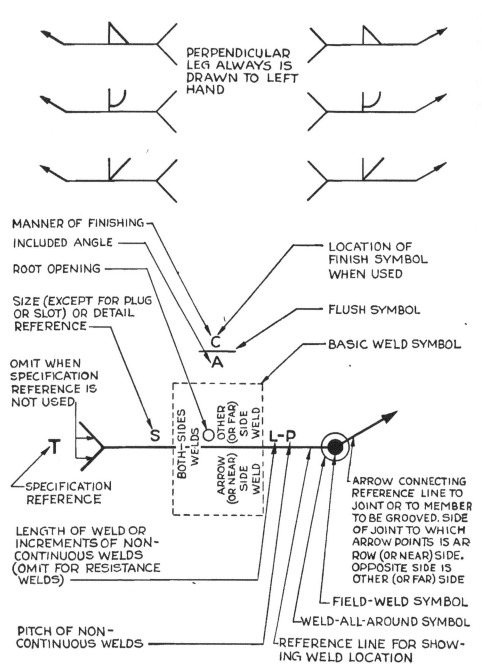

Fig. 50

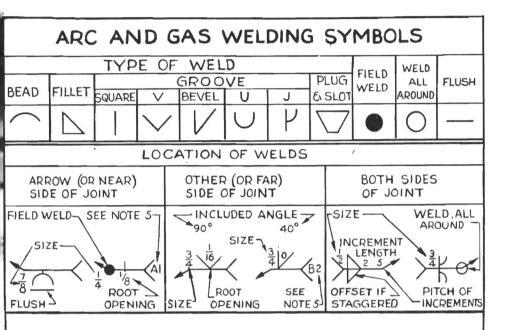

Fig. 51

1. THE SIDE OF THE JOINT TO WHICH THE ARROW POINTS IS THE ARROW (OR NEAR) SIDE

2. BOTH-SIDES WELDS OF SAME TYPE ARE OF SAME SIZE UNLESS OTHERWISE SHOWN

3. SYMBOLS APPLY BETWEEN ABRUPT CHANGES IN DIRECTION OF JOINT AS DIMENSIONED (EXCEPT WHERE ALL AROUND SYMBOL IS USED

4. ALL WELDS ARE CONTINUOUS AND OF USERS STANDARD PROPORTIONS, UNLESS OTHERWISE SHOWN

5 TAIL OF ARROW USED FOR SPECIFICATION REFERENCE (TAIL MAY BE OMITTED WHEN REFERENCE IS NOT USED)

6. DIMENSIONS OF WELD SIZES, INCREMENT LENGTHS AND SPACINGS IN INCHES

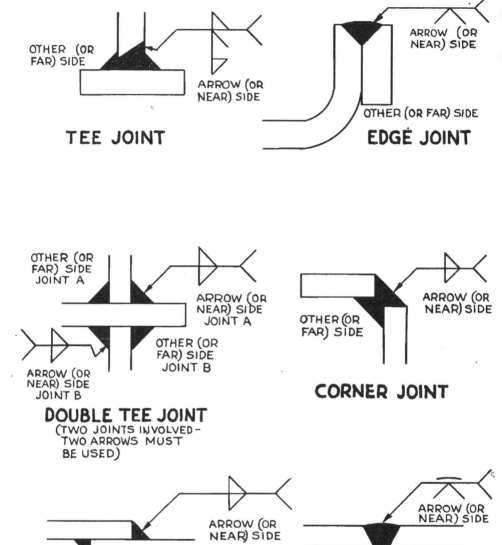

Fig. 52

red so that by using the assembly print is an easy matter to bring the finished rts together and assemble them into the ished unit. In some cases an assembly awing will be dimensioned. As such it comes a combined working and assembly awing and is used by tool and die makers d in some instances by the patternmaker. is often referred to as a "Tool Drawing" d generally details such objects as the rious jigs, punching, drilling, and tapng fixtures, and so on.

## stallation Drawings:

An installation or "location" drawing, as is sometimes called, is generally made for the use of the mechanic or millright in locating machinery and machiny drives in a manufacturing plant or achine shop. If the drawing concerns one iit it will generally show center-tonter distance of the mounting holes, cerin of the overall dimensions, height of ounting base from the floor, distance om the wall, etc. Or, if the installation nsists of several units, then in addition the above information the drawing will cely show all driving and driven shafts d drive belts on center lines and the disnces, either recommended or necessary, etween the units and from the walls of e building. The dimensions on such rawings generally represent distances om one unit to another. They do not sually detail parts of the unit except hen such dimensions are necessary in loating the machine. And as the dimensions enerally represent distances between and ot length and size of parts they are sually given in feet and inches for conenience.

## Ianufacturing Drawings:

When one manufacturer of a given product contracts with another to make certain arts of that product he usually supplies im with what are known as "manufacturg drawings." They are ordinary workg drawings supplemented with special ata, such as the steels, the heat-treat pecifications and often either designating e gages and checking instruments to be sed or listing these as the tools to be suplied along with the contracted work. Any ther necessary information, such as mateal lists, are usually placed on drawings.

## Welding Symbols:

With the development of welding as a means of speeding up the fabrication of both structural and machine parts there arose an immediate need for some means of conveying information from the designer to the welder quickly and accurately. Notations on drawings detailing welded parts became too involved and confusing for practical use. Hence an arrow symbol, Fig. 50, has been devised which presents the idea and specifications of the designer ideographically, that is, by means of graphic symbols. However, the arrow is only a part of the whole ideographic structure used in conveying welding information. As you can see from Fig. 51 there are a number of other symbols used in conjunction with the arrow. And inasmuch as each of these has, both of itself and of its position in relation to the arrow, a very definite significance, it will take some study to get the distinctions clearly in mind. Right away you will notice that the individual symbols, Fig. 51, can be compounded and connected with the arrow in such a way as to give the complete specification for complicated welding operations. In some work users will have need for only a few symbols and in certain cases they may originate legends or even symbols to suit their own special purposes. As we shall see later it is a quite common practice when the nature of the assembly permits, to place the symbols, legends, and specification references directly on the drawing instead of detailing the joints separately.

In Figs. 51 and 52 you will see the references "Arrow (or near) Side" and "Other (or far) Side" and at first these may be somewhat confusing due to the fact that the joints, Fig. 52, are shown in section, that is, you are looking at the joint cut in two edgewise. But if you keep in mind that the specifications always refer to the joint then the interpretation of the arrow side and the other (or far) side will perhaps be more clear. In Fig. 52 you will notice that some of the joints are completed from one side, the edge joint for example, where a V-weld completes the job. However, on the double-tee joint, corner joint, lap joint, etc., the weld is completed by working from both sides of a joined member, or in other words, "both-sides" welds are made. And notice particularly the arrows and the

## BUTT WELDS

### Fig. 53

| Section | Weld Symbol |
|---|---|

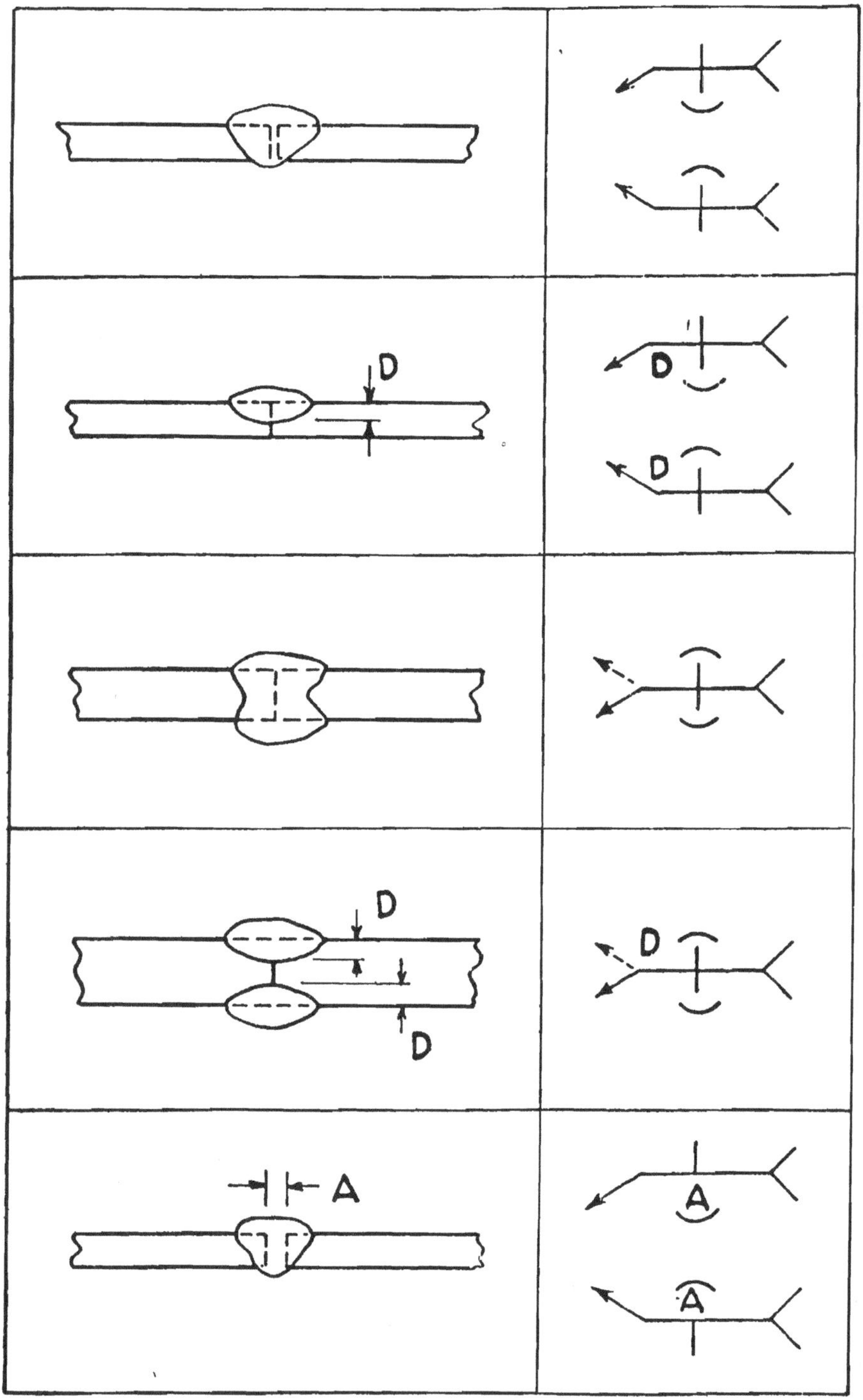

| Fig. 54 | Section | Weld Symbol |
|---|---|---|

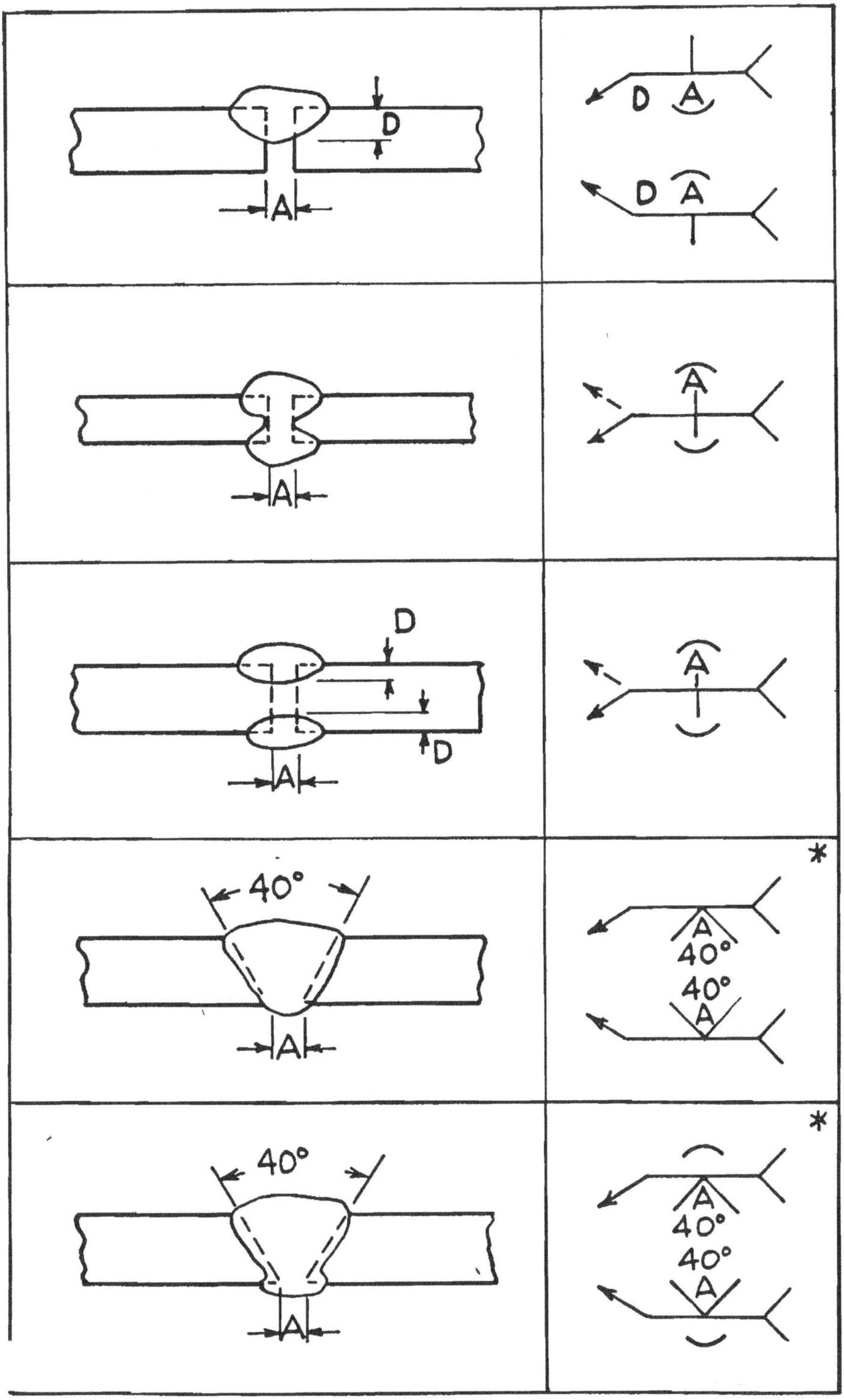

**Fig. 55**     Section           Weld Symbol

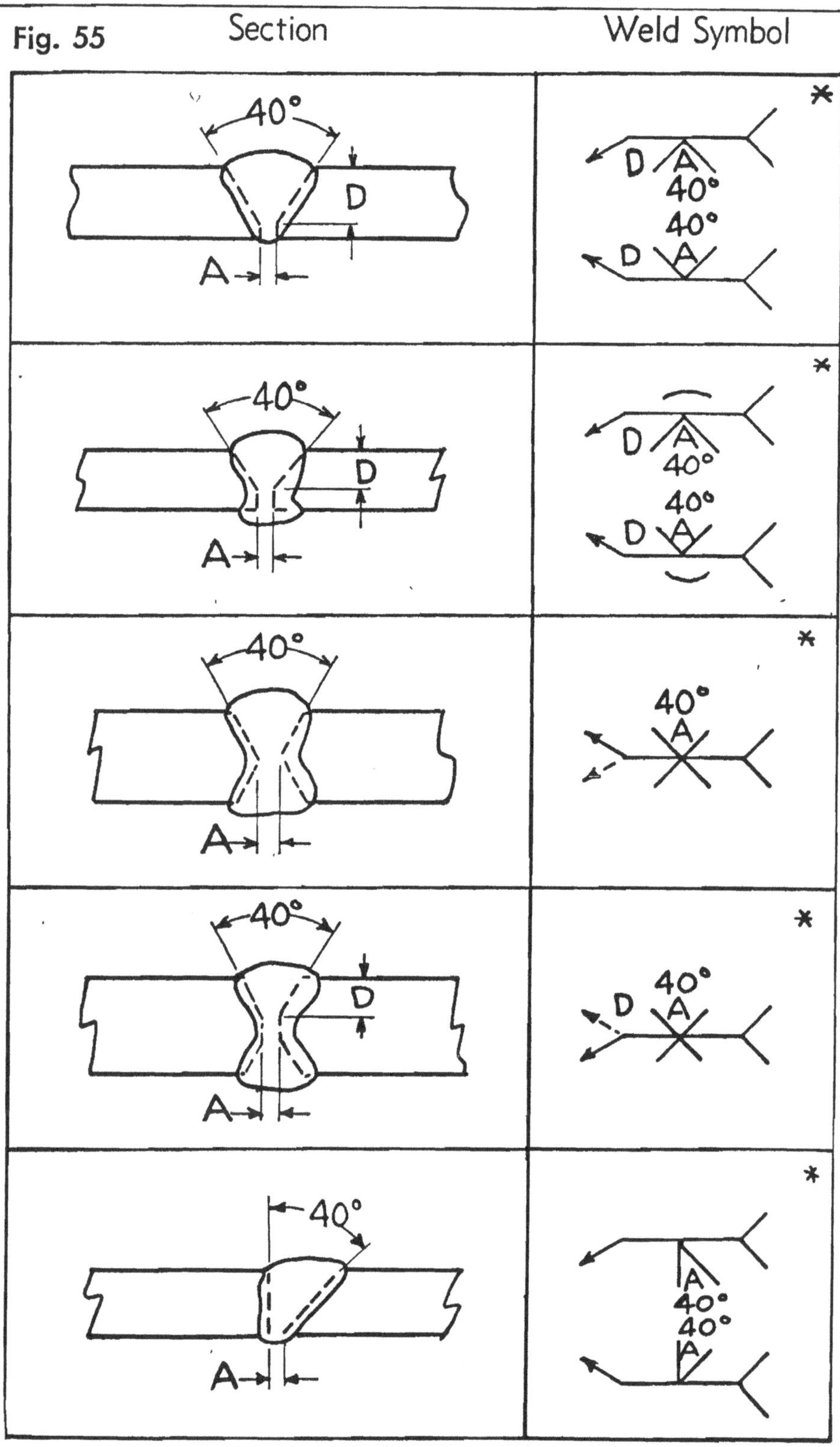

**Fig. 56**     Section                  Weld Symbol

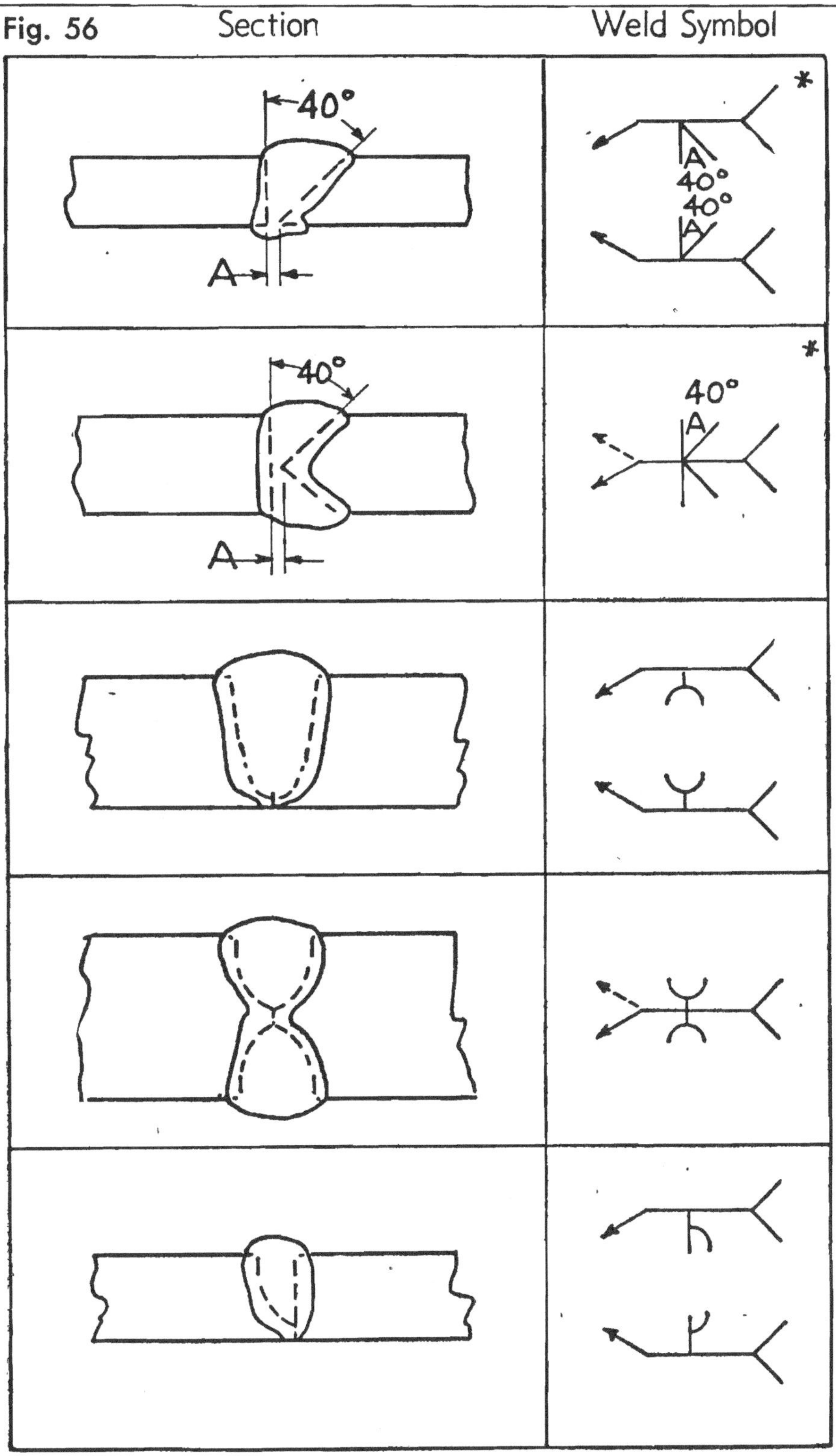

# CORNER JOINTS

## Fig. 57

Section                    Weld Symbol

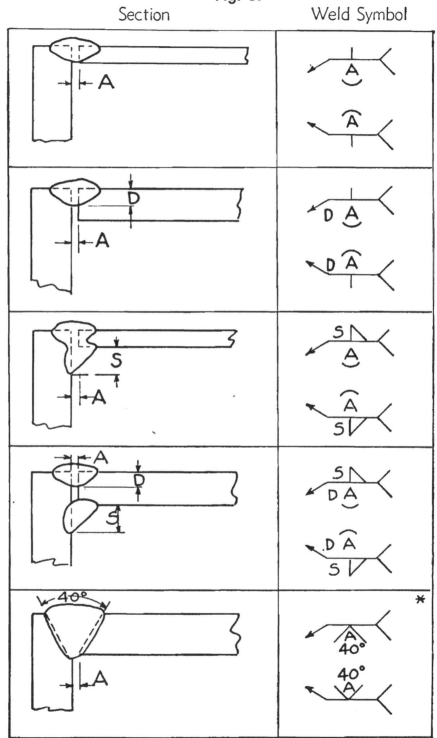

Fig. 58      Section            Weld Symbol

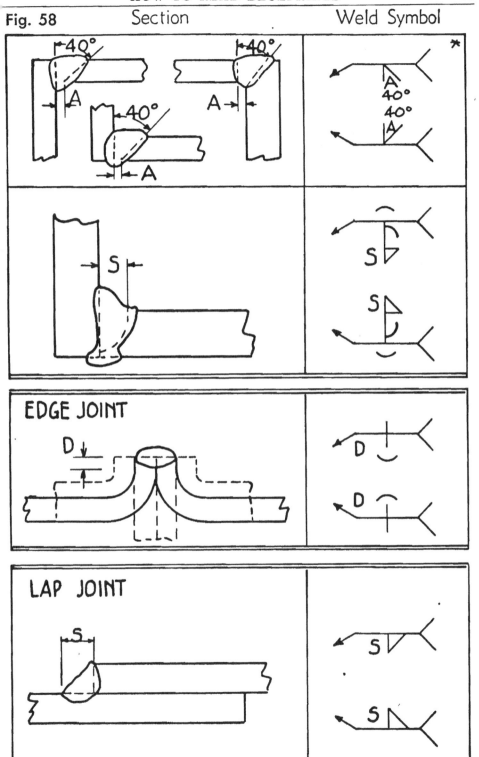

# TEE JOINTS

Fig. 59

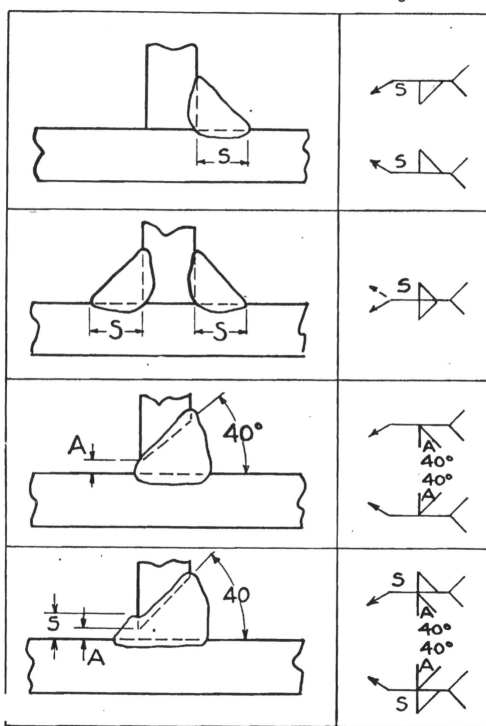

symbols on the joints just referred to. On the edge joint the arrow carries only the V-weld symbol and the symbol is placed below the arrow shaft or reference line, indicating a near-side weld. On all the other three the arrow carries symbols above and below the reference line indicating both near and far welds.

Figs. 53 to 59 inclusive show cross-sectional views of the various typical joints under the separate headings. In each case the symbol is shown with the joints. It should be remembered, too, that the combinations under each heading are numerous hence not nearly all the possible joints are shown. In all instances where an included angle of 40 degrees is indicated the specification is chosen merely for purposes of illustration. When shops adopt a standard included angle familiar to all concerned this specification is usually omitted from the symbol. Often this also is true of the root opening, as indicated by the letter "A" in the lower drawing, Fig. 53. The letter here is used for illustrative purposes only. Ordinarily, when the specification is necessary, it is given in inches or fractions thereof. Refer to Fig. 51. Now to look briefly at the variations in the butt welds beginning with those in Fig. 53. Notice first the variations in the perpendicular leg on the reference line of the arrows symbolizing the various operations. As you will see by referring to Fig. 51 this is the symbol for the "square" type of weld. In those views in Fig. 53 where letters are used, A refers to the root opening and B to the size of the weld. The tail of the arrow carries no specification reference in Figs. 53 to 59 inclusive but the tail is included for purposes of clarity. Where no reference is used the tail of the arrow can be omitted in actual practice. Refer to note 5 in Fig. 51. In Fig. 54 the three upper views, also all those in Fig. 53, show the meeting edges of the members to be square, but in the lower two views in Fig. 54 the meeting edges are beveled at an angle, the included angle being 40 degrees. Notice the change in the symbol indicating the type of weld. Following on through the two upper views in Fig. 55 only minor variations are indicated, but in the third and fourth views from the top the character of the weld changes. Here both sides of the joint are involved and the symbol for the V-weld

appears on both sides of the reference line. And finally, in the lower view in Fig. 55 the bevel-groove symbol turns up. Also, in the two top views in Fig. 56 are variations of the symbol. The lower three views in Fig. 56 show typical examples of the U and J-groove welds. By this time you will have noticed that the distinction between the symbols designating the V and bevel-groove welds and also the U and J-groove welds is not very great. For this reason it is necessary that the blueprint reader make a close study of any drawings involving use of these particular symbols especially when the symbol is not accompanied with a cross-sectional view of the joint, as is sometimes the case.

Fig. 57 and the two top views in Fig. 58 show common variations in the corner joint. Also compare the edge joint, lap joint, and tee joints, Figs. 58 and 59, with those corresponding in Fig. 52. From this elementary study of the arrow symbol and references it will be apparent that it provides a means of conveying a great amount of information from one person to another, that is, from the designer to the welder usually, with only a comparatively few lines, the position and type of which have much the same individual significance as ordinary shorthand. In fact, the numerical data and the words necessary to state fully the specifications for almost any common welded joint would require a fairly lengthy paragraph.

Thus far, no flush welds have been shown. The latter is indicated by a straight line across the symbol of the weld. Refer to Fig. 51. It means of course that the weld must be flush with the surface of the work when finished. The method of finishing flush is left to the operator in some instances but in most cases the blueprint carries a number of finish symbols, usually three letters, as in Fig. 60. Chipping, "C," usually means that the degree of finish is not at all critical and that those raised portions of the weld are to be chipped flush with the surrounding surface. Grinding, "G," can mean either rough or finish ground, and machining, "M," either rough or finish machined, as is the practice in the shop doing the work. It should be noted that the latter two symbols particularly do not distinguish between rough and finish grind or machine. Hence the quality or

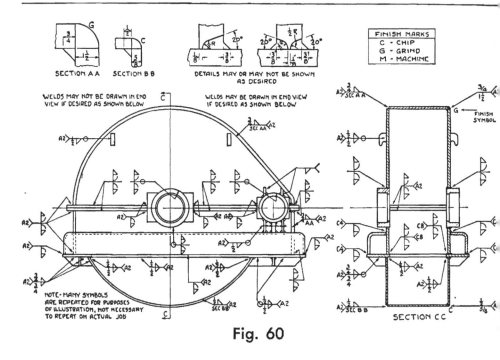

**Fig. 60**

degree of the finish must be determined either by the nature of the work, or by the practice of the individual shop.

Fig. 60 is a welded gear housing shown in front and sectional views in much the same fashion as you would see it arranged on a blueprint except that no parts are dimensioned. Certain notes have been added and symbols repeated in a number of instances for the sake of clarity. With a few minor changes this drawing could represent one of a type made especially for use of the welder. Of course the welder would not be particularly interested in the machining dimensions but he would be very much concerned with all those dimensions and data pertaining to assembly and welding, as very frequently he is furnished with ready-formed pieces to weld into a complete assembly. The notes in Fig. 60 referring to drawing of the welds in end view and the repetition of symbols are explanatory only. These notes do not usually appear on the shop drawing unless they or similar notes are required for some special reason. Sometimes the drawing will include the symbols legend, Fig. 51, and any special information along with it that is considered necessary.

In any study of blueprint reading one

should keep in mind that it is likely there will be still further simplifications in the manner of presenting the various common objects such as threads, springs, gears, etc. In fact, many simplifications are now under consideration, but as yet are only in the tentative stage.

And finally, it can be said that the student may well regard his study of blueprint reading and related subjects as the "ABCs" of his machine-shop course. Every effort should be made to supplement this study with careful observation of machining operations, machine parts and machine assemblies. Familiarity with the common functions of machine parts and their assembly into finished units comes only with intensive study. It is essentially a part of the process of self-improvement, of acquiring a background of practical knowledge. In this way an understanding of the essentials of blueprint reading becomes a basis for future education and advancement.

Several of the instructional drawings pertaining to Lines, Threads and Dimensions have been abstracted from the American Standards publication, "Drawings and Drafting Room Practice" Z14 1, available from American Standards Association, 29 West 39th Street, New York City

Figs 27, 28 and 34 to 44 inclusive reprinted from Machinery's Handbook by courtesy of the publishers, The Industrial Press, 140 Lafayette Street, New York City

Figs 50, 51 and 53 to 60 inclusive reprinted by courtesy of the Lincoln Electric Company, Cleveland, Ohio.

# Helpful Aids in Making and Storing Blueprints

Here is a dispenser for handling blueprint and other sensitized paper that speeds cutting to length and at the same time prevents the paper from being exposed to light. It consists of a rectangular box 4½ by 36 in. inside dimensions, with a hinged side, and a felt gasket, which keeps light out and permits the paper to be drawn through smoothly. Fastened to the top of the box is a razor blade which cuts the paper quickly and evenly. Only a small strip about ½ in. wide is left exposed to the light. The box may be nailed up out of ½ by 4½-in. pine and the guide for the cutter out of two small strips rabbeted on the edge and nailed to a piece of ¼-in. plywood. The whole assembly can be fastened to the underside of a table and the paper may be drawn out over the top and cut to size with a minimum of waste. By changing the dimensions, the design easily may be made for any size roll. The same type of dispenser is also useful in handling tracing and drawing paper.

### Weather Strip Stops T-Square Sliding

To prevent a T-square from sliding too easily on your drawing board, nail a length of rubber weather stripping on the left-hand edge of the board at such height that the cross-piece of the square will rest upon it when the blade is pressed against the board. The friction of the rubber will hold it firmly and eliminate much of the usual arm and finger strain.

¶A number of parallel lines can be made at one time by holding steel pen points in a spring paper clip. All the pens must be of the same size, although the type of points may vary.

### Can Lids Protect Ends of Blueprints

Rolls of blueprints are protected against damage at the ends if baking-powder can lids are used as shown. Holes are punched in opposite sides of each lid to attach rubber bands, which

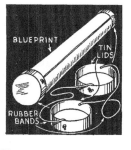

hold them on the roll. As the lids are easy to remove and replace, workmen are not likely to neglect referring to the plans frequently as is often the case with less convenient containers.

### Fixing Bath for Blueprints

A concentrated solution of peroxide of hydrogen mixed with water makes a good bath in which to fix blueprints. The proper mixture is peroxide of hydrogen, 1 or 2 oz., liquid measure, to a 4 by 5-ft. washing tank carrying a water level of about 4 in. The solution need not be drained off each day as it will be perfectly good as a fixing bath for two or three days. Its strength does not diminish but it must be drained off, due to sludge from the paper coating. Blueprints that have been fixed in this bath have a deep blue background and the lines are perfectly white. Also, it is unnecessary for the operator to use gloves.—L. H. Georger, Buffalo, N. Y.

### Drawing Large Hexagon Figures

When you want to draw large hexagon figures, and there is no compass or square at hand, use a castellated nut. Using the

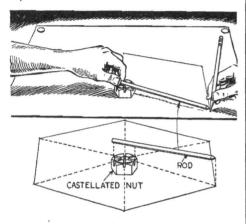

nut as a center, place a rod, pencil or similar object in two slots of the nut and mark the work at the end of the rod. Repeat this operation for each of the six slots, taking care that the rod projects the same distance from the nut each time. Connecting the marks with lines completes the figure.—W. C. Wilhite, Carlinville, Ill.

### Improving Drafting Triangle

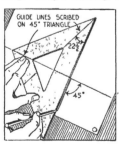

By scribing two or three lines at different angles on a transparent triangle, you can instantly place it in a position to draw lines at various angles. First, scribe a line at right angles to the long side. Now, when you want to draw a line at an angle of 45 degrees from one already drawn, place the triangle on the

work so that the scribed line is directly above the one on the work. Other lines can be scribed at different angles.

### Washers Hold Blueprint Flat

Difficulty of keeping a blueprint spread on a bench or table may be eliminated by attaching a small metal washer at each corner with gummed-paper tape, as indicated.

### Restoring Faded Blueprints

Blueprints that have been rushed through the washing process to get them on the job quickly, often fade on contact with strong light. If this happens, store them in a dark place a few hours and their original color will return.

### Pencils Held on Drawing Board

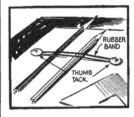

Stretched across one corner of a drawing board and fastened at the ends with thumb tacks, an ordinary rubber band provides a good emergency pencil holder. Just slip the pencils under the rubber band which will keep them from rolling.

### Clamp on T-Square Grips Edge of Board

Draftsmen, artists and others will welcome this method of holding a T-square head to the edge of the board while working with triangles. From a piece of heavy cardboard or thin wood, cut a strip about 1¼ in. wide and 6 in. long. In the center of this, make a slot to slip over the T-square snugly. In use, place the T-square on the drawing board in the desired position, slip the piece of cardboard or thin wood over it, pulling it snugly against the edge of the drawing board. Then slip two large paper clips of the clamp type over the edges of the T-square to hold the cardboard tightly against the edge of the board.

## Metal Holder for Blueprints

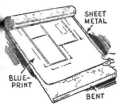

While on a job, one contractor protects his blueprints by keeping them in portable holders which are nothing more than pieces of sheet metal bent as indicated. In use, the print is inserted so that it can be pulled out for inspection or pushed back so that it rolls up inside the tubular part of the holder.

## Clip Holds Drawing-Ink Bottle Cork

If the quill on the cork of a drawing-ink bottle is not used and the bottle must be kept open while lettering or writing with an ordinary pen, there is no need to lay the cork on the table or on your work,

which may result in an ink stain. Just bend a narrow strip of brass double and spread it to fit the bottle neck and to take the cork. A length of wire could be substituted for the brass strip if desired.

## Paddle Avoids Soiling of Blueprints

Small plans or blueprints and even magazine pages containing drawings can be held on a plywood paddle for easy reference at the workbench. In this way, the paper does not have to be touched with soiled hands. Notches at each corner of the pad-

dle permit rubber bands to be slipped over the corners of the paper to keep it in place.

## Tracings Stored in Window Shades

A number of window shades with their rollers mounted between vertical supports as shown, provide handy places for storing

blueprints, unfinished tracings, and similar work. In use, a shade is unrolled, the tracing or blueprint laid on it and rolled up with the shade.

## Tack Holder on Drawing Board

Half of a hollow rubber ball provides a handy thumbtack tray on a drawing board. Flexibility of the rubber makes it easy to select and remove the tacks.

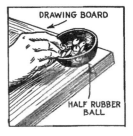

## Shop Prints Protected With Tin Backing

Instead of pasting shop drawings and blueprints on a piece of cardboard to help protect them, one foreman mounts them on a sheet of tin. A good paste for this purpose is made by stirring rice flour into boiling water until the mixture thickens, after which glycerine, 1 oz., is added for each pint of paste, and thoroughly mixed. This paste is adherent and will not peel from the tin. After the drawings have been mounted and allowed to dry, they are given a coat of clear, waterproof varnish.

## Pencil Pointer Swings Under Board

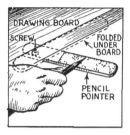

Rather than have a sandpaper pencil pointer lying on his drawing board, where it is likely to soil papers, one draftsman finds a piece of sandpaper glued to a strip of wood and pivoted to the underside of the drawing board handy. The pointer swings under the board out of the way when not in use so that there is no possibility of it soiling the draftsman's work.

## Tabs on Prints Prevent Finger Smudges

Annoyed by blueprints being soiled when handled by various workmen, a Wisconsin contractor attached paper tabs to the corners of the prints for handling them. The tabs are held firmly in place with paper clips of the type shown.

## Blueprints Sprayed With Lacquer

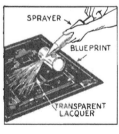

Immediately after getting blueprints for a job, an Arizona contractor applies a thin coating of transparent lacquer to them with a small insect sprayer. He claims that this waterproofs the prints, gives them a tough coating which makes them tear-resistant, and also permits them to be cleaned easily with a damp cloth.

## Ink Bottle Kept Upright by Holder

The problem of keeping an ink bottle in a vertical position on a drawing board was solved with this simple holder, which can be made from thin sheet metal or a

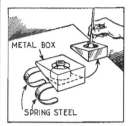

small tin box. If the latter is used, remove the bottom and taper the sides so that they are about one third as wide at one end as at the other. Then solder the bottom in place, and rivet two spring-steel clips to it, bending them as indicated in the drawing, to slip over the board.

## Stovepipe Case Carries Blueprints

A length of stovepipe makes a good container and carrying case for blueprints. A regular metal handle is riveted in the center of the pipe as indicated. Thus the unit is

easy to handle, and because of the metal, the prints are well protected.

—Opie Read, Jr., Chicago.

## Fuller Ball as Instrument Handle

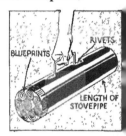

Drawing tools, especially compasses and dividers, may be made much more convenient for use if a fuller ball, about ½ in. in diameter, is forced over the handle of each. This gives a large, non-slip grip.

## Blueprint Paper Made at Home

Satisfactory blueprint paper can be made at home with the following solution: In one bottle, dissolve ammonium citrate of iron, 3¾ oz., in water, 18 oz., and then dissolve red prussiate of potash, 2⅝ oz., in the ame quantity of water, in another bottle. Have the paper to be treated close at and in a photographic dark room lighted nly by a ruby light. Mix equal parts of the solutions and apply with a sponge. Put the liquid on in long parallel sweeps and on one side of the paper only. Hang the sheets up to dry and keep them in the dark until used. The mixtures spoil very quickly, so it is advisable to throw away that which is not used, rather than keep it for future use.

## Sponge Rubber Cleans Triangle

Edges of triangles and other drawing instruments may be cleaned quickly merely by pulling them across a small piece of sponge rubber attached near the upper right-hand corner of the drawing board. When a drafting job has been completed, the sponge should be removed and washed in warm water to remove ink.

## Blueprint Files Resemble Boiler Flues

A sheet-metal contracting firm in Omaha, Nebr., has a file for its blueprints that resembles the flue system of a boiler. Sheet metal was used to form supports for metal tubes, which were left open at the ends. With the tubes marked in alphabetical order, filing and finding blueprints is comparatively easy. This method also keeps the prints nicely rolled and well protected from dust or other damage.

## Scale on Edge of French Curve

When you have a drawing that requires the making of duplicate curves, a scale on the edge of your French curve will

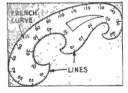

aid greatly in this work. Equally spaced lines are scored on the curve, then every tenth one is numbered. Ink applied to the scored lines makes them easy to see.

## Rubber Bands on Print Save Time

By permanently attaching rubber bands to blueprints, a contractor saved time because the bands could not be misplaced when a print was unrolled. Strips of adhesive tape held the bands in place.

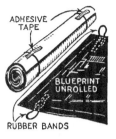

## Handy Scale for Edge of Drawing Board

You won't have to stop work and look for a ruler that has been misplaced, if you set a scale in the surface of your drawing board near the edge as indicated. The scale can be any length desired within the limits of the board, and should be set flush with the surface. The recess for the scale should be cut carefully on the edge of the board that is used the least so that it does not interfere with use of the T-square.

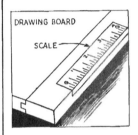

## Washer Prevents Tearing Paper

When using thin tracing paper on a drawing board, clip a large cardboard washer under the head of each thumbtack. This provides a larger bearing surface on the paper so that the head of the tack is less likely to tear the paper.

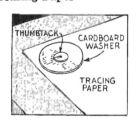

## Waterproofing Solution for Blueprints

To waterproof blueprints and give them a sheen and greater legibility, rub them with a soft cloth that has been dampened with a solution of rosin, 50 grains, paraffin, 100 grains, and turpentine, 1 oz.

¶When it is necessary to fold a blueprint, back the creases with adhesive tape and the print will last longer.

# INDEX

CPSIA information can be obtained at www.ICGtesting.com
Printed in the USA
LVOW010543021212

309688LV00003B/492/P

3 1143 00976 5661

9 781258 179502